MRCP 2

Passing The

PACES

PASTEST

Dedicated to your success

MRCP 2

Passing The

PACES

Julian A. Gray MA DPhil MRCP(UK)
CEO, Neutris Pharmaceuticals LLC

and

Andrew V. Thillainayagam MD FRCP
Consultant and Honorary Senior
Lecturer in Medicine
Gastroenterology Unit
Hammersmith Hospitals NHS Trust
London

© 2002 PASTEST LTD
Egerton Court
Parkgate Estate
Knutsford
Cheshire WA16 8DX

Telephone: 01565 752000

First published in 1986 as *MRCP 2 Preparation for the clinical*
Revised edition first published in 2002
Reprinted 2003, 2004

ISBN 1 901198 73 1

A catalogue record for this book is available from the British Library.

The information contained within this book was obtained by the author from reliable sources. However, while every effort has been made to ensure its accuracy, no responsibility for loss, damage or injury occasioned to any person acting or refraining from action as a result of information contained herein can be accepted by the publishers or author.

PasTest Revision Books and Intensive Courses
PasTest has been established in the field of postgraduate medical education since 1972, providing revision books and intensive study courses for doctors preparing for their professional examinations.
Books and courses are available for the following specialties:
MRCP Part 1 and Part 2, MRCPCH Part 1 and Part 2, MRCS, MRCOG, MRCGP, DRCOG, MRCPsych, DCH, FRCA and PLAB.
For further details contact:
PasTest Ltd, Freepost, Knutsford, Cheshire WA16 7BR
Tel: 01565 752000   Fax: 01565 650264
E-mail: enquiries@pastest.co.uk
Web site: www.pastest.co.uk

Typeset by Breeze Ltd, Manchester.
Printed by Athenaeum Press Ltd, Tyne and Wear.

CONTENTS

FOREWORD

The clinical section of the MRCP examination is the part which many candidates fear the most. All too often candidates have prepared in the wrong way. Then, with the added stress of being observed and questioned by eminent physicians, it is only too easy to look uncertain and unprofessional and to utter statements which even to your own ears sound wrong or even ridiculous. Thus, many candidates fail themselves: a thoroughly miserable experience which can generally be avoided by careful and thoughtful preparation.

This book is not intended to teach you medicine: you should know this already. Instead, it is a guide on how to prepare for, and hence pass, the clinical examination.

The original version of this book has been revised to take into account the introduction of the new MRCP Part 2 clinical examination: PACES (Practical Assessment of Clinical Examination Skills).

In the new examination the short cases have been retained but the long case and viva have been replaced by standardised assessments of history taking and of the candidate's communications skills and knowledge of and approach to issues involving medical ethics.

The text focuses on the short cases, with proposed schemes of examination and examples of common cases including those mentioned in the Royal College's *Guidelines to PACES*. The latter is mandatory reading for candidates and includes vital information about the examination itself and the marking scheme used.

New chapters have been added on history taking, communication skills and ethics.

In updating the text I am delighted to have been joined by my former teaching colleague on the Guildford MRCP course, Dr Andrew Thillainayagam.

Julian Gray
London 2002

1. PREPARING FOR THE CLINICAL

1.1   Examination format

The clinical part of the MRCP Part 2 examination is called PACES –
Practical Assessment of Clinical Examination Skills. Each candidate is
examined at five 'Stations' which deal with different types of clinical cases
as follows (see MRCP(UK) PACES guidelines (see p. 168) for further details):

Station 1: Respiratory and Abdominal Systems

Candidates examine and discuss short cases on the abdominal and
respiratory systems (10 minutes for each system, total 20 minutes).

Station 2: History Taking

The candidate's history taking skills are assessed during a 15 minute
history taking session with a patient in the presence of two examiners.
After the history taking the patient leaves the station and there is 5 minutes
of discussion of the case with the examiners.

Station 3: Cardiovascular and Neurological Systems

Candidates examine and discuss short cases on the cardiovascular and
neurological systems (10 minutes for each system, total 20 minutes).

Station 4: Communication Skills and Ethics

The candidate's ability to guide and organise an interview with the subject,
provide emotional support, discuss further management and handle
ethical issues is assessed during a 15 minute interaction with a patient or
relative in the presence of two examiners. After this the patient or relative
leaves the station and there is a five minute discussion of the case with the
two examiners.

Station 5: Skin, Locomotor system, Eyes and Endocrine System

Candidates examine and discuss short cases concerning the skin,
locomotor system, eyes and endocrine system (5 minutes for each system,
total 20 minutes).

THE PACES CAROUSEL

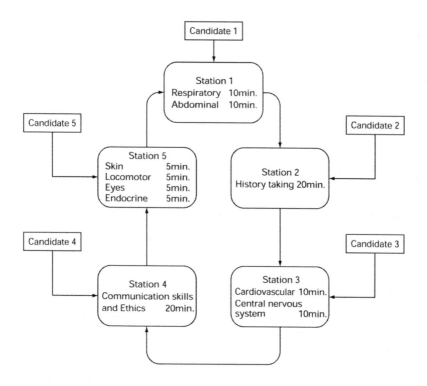

1.2   General advice

History Taking, Communication Skills and Ethics

Assuming you are in a busy medical job, these sections are likely to present little difficulty as they present situations which you will be encountering on a daily basis. However, it is important to rehearse for these sections with a fellow candidate, and more detailed advice is given in the relevant chapters below.

Short cases

The short cases remain for most candidates the most difficult part of the examination and you must devote considerable preparation time to it. Examining short cases is a skill which can only be mastered by careful preparation and repeated rehearsal. The situation is unusually stressful due to the presence of two examiners who know the correct diagnosis, the fact that you cannot ask questions of the patient and the time limit set.

You should devise and commit to memory a scheme for examination of the different systems and selected short cases. Suggested methods for this are set out in the respective chapters but should be modified to your own taste. Most of your practising, however, should be done on the wards seeing patients as you would in the examination.

Indeed, the essence of preparation boils down to one thing: *you must make yourself examine patients repeatedly in front of an observer.* Here to team up with a like-minded candidate is critically important. Not only is this more fun than working alone but it is infinitely more effective. You will be surprised at how much more difficult it is to perform well when being watched, even by someone you know. You must get used to this as early as possible. In our opinion, practising alone is virtually useless.

You should take it in turns to play the role of the examiner: a most valuable exercise in itself as it gives insight into the sort of questions which are likely to be asked.

You should also persuade a senior colleague with recent experience of the examination to take you round a series of 'unseen' cases on a regular basis. For maximum benefit, these sessions should be kept as realistic as possible, with the 'examiner' behaving in a suitably cool and neutral manner. Any discussion about how you are getting on should be left until the end of the whole session. This will give you experience of the difficulty of seeing several different cases in quick succession and of keeping going even if you have made a mistake.

Use your polished examination techniques, with no short cuts, in the clinics and on the wards at all times.

With time and perseverance you will start to notice improvement in your performance. This should lead to an increase in your self-confidence: you will not pass the examination without a reasonable amount of this.

Finally, if you are approaching your preparation correctly you should find that you are actually deriving some enjoyment from it. Both the sharpening of your clinical skills and the element of gamesmanship involved can be very stimulating. If you feel miserable *all* the time there must be something fundamentally wrong with your approach!

1.3   Short case technique

According to the marking scheme, which has now been standardised and described in the MRCP PACES guidebook[1], you will be examined on the following items:

- Physical examination – technique and thoroughness of the examination (described in more detail below for each system examined)
- Identification and interpretation of physical signs – leading to the correct diagnosis
- Discussion related to the case – including relevant investigations and sequence, and appropriate further therapy and management

---

[1] *MRCP (UK) Part 2 Clinical Examination (PACES) and Clinical Guidelines 2001/2* edition, MRCP(UK) Central Office, Royal College of Physicians of the United Kingdom

You will receive written instructions as to what is required of you. For example:

'This 60-year-old man has had increasing shortness of breath for the past five years. Examine his respiratory system and try to establish the cause'.

Whatever the request, you should start by shaking hands with, and introducing yourself to, the patient and by asking him whether he minds if you examine him. You must of course be courteous and respectful to the patient however nervous you are feeling! Make sure, with the patient's permission, that the patient is undressed adequately to allow a complete examination of the system specified. Adequate exposure can reveal all sorts of hidden clues: biopsy scars in the groin and neck are classical examples, as are thyroidectomy scars. It is not unheard of for your approach to be tested in this way. For example, you might be asked to examine the chest in an elderly lady who has had a stroke. The important point is not to compromise: you must arrange the patient in the correct position with the chest exposed so that you can perform a thorough examination, despite all the practical difficulties involved.

At this point the unprepared usually forget one important act: *observation*. Observing the patient need not take more than a few seconds but will impress the examiners and will quite often give you the diagnosis. Be certain that the examiners see you stand back and observe the patient. Do not forget to look for clues by the patient's bed, such as a bottle of diabetic orange juice or a salbutamol inhaler.

All the steps of the examination should be clear to the onlookers and follow on quickly and smoothly from one another. Repeated practice is the only way to do this and those who have done this can be recognised within seconds of starting their examination of a patient. Schemes of examination for the different systems have been included in the chapters for the different PACES stations. No method of examination is 'correct' and you should modify these methods so that they feel natural to you in practice and can be performed smoothly and automatically even when under stress.

When you have finished examining each case, be sure to thank the patient and to help them to put their clothes back on.

Presenting your findings

As soon as you straighten up from examining the patient you will be asked 'What did you find?'

There are two ways of presenting your findings:

(i) **If you are sure of the diagnosis** you should state this, followed by your reasons. An example would be:

'This patient has Parkinson's disease, as shown by a coarse pill-rolling tremor of the hands at rest, cogwheel rigidity of the arms, ...' etc.

This method of presentation has many advantages; not only does it make you sound confident, but it also gives you much more control over what you include and what you omit from your presentation. There are times when it is better not to mention signs about which you are not sure; to some extent, everything which you say can be used in evidence against you!

(ii) **If you are not sure of the diagnosis** you should go through your findings methodically and at the end give a probable diagnosis or differential diagnosis. Do not lose your nerve or apologise for not knowing the diagnosis; often this is not actually expected of you. Many cases are chosen to test your clinical approach rather than your ability to 'spot the diagnosis'. There are times when to be too definite can stand against you. For example, you might be shown a patient with jaundice and a firm enlarged liver. It would be wrong to say 'This patient has hepatic secondaries'. This should certainly enter into your differential diagnosis, but to give it as a firm diagnosis would indicate lack of experience.

You will commonly be asked to discuss which investigations you would perform. Remember to start with simple investigations before moving to more complex – and expensive – ones. You will also likely be asked to discuss the management of the case. Again, mention general and supportive measures before drug treatments as appropriate.

A short case variant is to be asked to examine a specific region 'and anything else which you feel is relevant'. If you have prepared properly, your mind should already be thinking of these associations in any case, as I will now describe.

1.4 Mastering the case

The membership will always be a competitive examination, with candidates before and after you being tested on the same patients. To impress your examiners you should consider how to take your examination one step further after you have reached a diagnosis. Planning this aspect should be a stimulating and enjoyable exercise.

To illustrate this, let us take the following example. You are asked to examine the hands in a patient with obvious rheumatoid arthritis (a common short case). The immediate reaction is to breathe a sigh of relief because at last you will be able to give a confident diagnosis. Unfortunately, so could a first year medical student! It is these cases which call for the slickest performance and the ability to examine the case in greater depth than that of the average candidate. In the case of rheumatoid hands, for example, you would make a good impression (after a thorough examination of the various features of the disease) by performing some simple bedside tests of function, such as doing up buttons or writing. This indicates a practical approach to the patient's disability.

Similarly, having diagnosed mitral stenosis you should look for and comment on the presence or absence of complications of the condition rather than letting the examiners drag this information out of you.

1.5 Planning your revision

As already stated, the only way to master the technique of handling short cases is to practise them repeatedly in front of someone on the wards. However, there is also a lot to be gained by planning out on paper your method of tackling different short case situations, especially those which crop up regularly.

It is worthwhile making lists of the signs that accompany the various conditions which occur as short cases. There are many books available to help you do this but be sure to make your own lists because you will remember much better information you have written down yourself.

This method of preparation has one important limitation: although some short cases are immediately recognisable 'from the end of the bed', on many occasions this is not so, and the diagnosis only becomes clear at the end of the examination, if at all! On those lucky occasions when the diagnosis *is* obvious it certainly helps to be able to switch into a prepared routine of examination as for example with rheumatoid arthritis or Parkinson's disease. For the other occasions, it is vital to be absolutely systematic about your method of examination. You must prepare and rehearse a method of examining each system of the body. Your normal methods will probably need to be adjusted and 'race-tuned' for the rigours of the short cases. Not only must your technique be smooth and well polished, but you must also incorporate certain safety checks such as feeling both radial pulses to avoid being caught out by an absent radial.

To help you with this aspect of your preparation suggested schemes of examination have been compiled at the beginning of the respective chapters on the different stations.

1.6 Equipment to take with you

Before you start your preparation you should make sure that you possess a complete set of reliable diagnostic instruments. It is not worth economising over this: it is a great advantage in the clinical to be using equipment with which you have practised and feel at home.

It is suggested that you keep the following in your 'armoury':

- Stethoscope
- Watch with a second hand
- Ophthalmoscope
- Pen torch (with new batteries)
- Tendon hammer, with long handle and *soft* rubber end
- Red and white hat pins: head should be 5 mm diameter
- Tuning fork
- Cotton wool
- Orange sticks (for testing plantar responses)
- Wooden spatulae
- Tape measure
- Pocket ruler
- Pocket-sized reading chart (for testing visual acuity)

2. STATION 1 – THE RESPIRATORY AND ABDOMINAL SYSTEMS

2.1 THE RESPIRATORY SYSTEM

SCHEME OF EXAMINATION OF RESPIRATORY SYSTEM

'Examine the respiratory system'

Action	Notes
Introduce yourself and ask permission to examine the patient	
Position patient comfortably in upright sitting position with chest fully undressed	
Check bedside locker for sputum pot and inspect this if present	
Look quickly at hands for clubbing or peripheral cyanosis	
Feel radial pulse and count respiratory rate	*? rapid, bounding pulse of CO_2 retention, check for flapping tremor if you suspect this*
Glance at pupils and conjunctivae	*? Horner's syndrome* *? anaemic/polycythaemic*
Look at tongue	*? central cyanosis*
Stand at end of bed and observe while patient breathes in	*? scars; deformities* *? asymmetrical expansion* *? evidence of radiotherapy e.g. telangiectasia* *? engorged superficial veins (e.g. SVC obstruction)* *? paradoxical movement of abdomen (e.g. phrenic nerve palsy)*
Further assess expansion anteriorly by palpation	

Palpate trachea and apex beat

Percuss chest anteriorly   *Do not forget to percuss over the clavicles*

Palpate for tactile fremitus

Auscultate anteriorly, including over the apices

If crepitations are heard ask the patient to cough, then repeat the auscultation; ask yourself whether they are fine or coarse crepitations and early or end inspiratory

Auscultate for vocal resonance anteriorly

Ask patient to sit forward

Assess expansion posteriorly by palpation

Percuss posteriorly, including the axillae

When consolidation is suspected, check for additional signs such as increased vocal resonance, whispering pectoriloquy and aegophony

Palpate for tactile fremitus

Auscultate posteriorly, including axillae

Auscultate for vocal resonance posteriorly

Palpate for cervical, supraclavicular and axillary lymphadenopathy

NB. You may be asked to comment on **appearance of sputum** (e.g. copious mucopurulent sputum in bronchiectasis. You must also be able to elicit **measurement of peak flow rate** using a peak flow meter and be able to assess **inhaler technique**.

POPULAR SHORT CASES ON THE RESPIRATORY SYSTEM

CHRONIC BRONCHITIS/EMPHYSEMA

This is a common short case and you must have a method of examination fully prepared in order to be able to shine.

- Always start by examining the sputum pot

- Look at the nails for nicotine staining or clubbing (the later suggests pathology other than emphysema or chronic bronchitis)

- Feel the hands and pulse for signs of carbon dioxide retention (e.g. warm hands, rapid bounding pulse)

- Look at the face and conjunctivae for plethora, and at the underside of the tongue and vermilion border of the lip for central cyanosis

- Observe the patient from the end of the bed: count the respiratory rate and look for purse-lip breathing

- Examine carefully for evidence of hyperinflation of the chest:

  - Symmetrical diminution of chest expansion
  - Increased A-P diameter of the chest (but note this may also occur in disorders of the thoracic spine)
  - Use of accessory muscles of respiration, especially the sterno-cleidomastoids (also scaleni, trapezii)
  - Indrawing of intercostal spaces, supraclavicular fossae and costal margins on inspiration
  - Shortening of the distance between the cricoid cartilage and the suprasternal notch to less than three finger breadths
  - Loss of cardiac and hepatic dullness. The apex beat may be impalpable (other causes are obesity, pericardial effusion, dextrocardia).
  - Hyperresonance of the chest on percussion

The breath sounds may be quiet: remember that early inspiratory crackles especially at the bases, frequently occur in chronic bronchitis, as do expiratory wheezes.

Look for elevation of the jugular venous pulse and ankle oedema which may suggest right-sided heart failure (cor pulmonale).

Try to decide whether your patient fits into the category of 'pink puffer' or 'blue bloater' (see chart below) or whether he has features of both. If you suspect CO_2 retention, ask if you may examine the fundi for papilloedema, and test for flapping tremor of the outstretched hands.

	'Pink Puffer'	'Blue Bloater'
Build	Thin	Obese
Cyanosis	-	+
Breathlessness	++	+
Hyperinflation of chest	+++	+
Cor pulmonale	-	+ (often)

Notes

BRONCHIECTASIS

This condition is quite commonly shown as a short case. There may be evidence of copious sputum production, sometimes blood-stained, in the sputum pot on the bedside locker: always inspect this first.

The patient is often clubbed.

The characteristic finding is of coarse, leathery crackles, often over the bases; during acute exacerbations there may be a pleural rub.

If you are reasonably confident of the diagnosis you may go on to look for dextrocardia (present, with sinusitis, in Kartagener's syndrome) and ask whether you may examine for features of secondary amyloidosis (e.g. hepatosplenomegaly).

Revise the causes of the condition, but remember to mention common causes like childhood measles or whooping cough and cystic fibrosis before rarer ones such as hypogammaglobulinaemia.

Notes

FIBROSING ALVEOLITIS

This is a popular short case, with which you must be familiar.

The patient is usually clubbed. In advanced cases central cyanosis is present at rest. Chest expansion is limited and the percussion note may be dull over the lower thorax due to elevation of the diaphragm as the lung volume shrinks.

The hallmark of the disease is the presence of showers of bilateral fine basal crackles in late inspiration; characteristically they become quieter or disappear when the patient leans forward. Unlike the crackles of pulmonary oedema (which may also be late inspiratory) they do not clear on coughing; test for this.

Look for evidence of pulmonary hypertension (loud P_2, 'a' waves in jugular venous pulse, left parasternal heave) and cor pulmonale (raised JVP, tender hepatomegaly, peripheral oedema). Note that these occur only late in the disease course.

Occasionally there will be evidence of diseases associated with fibrosing alveolitis (e.g. rheumatoid arthritis, systemic lupus erythematosus, systemic sclerosis, dermatomyositis (see Medicine International Vol.1 1982. No.22 p.1020 A Johnson). Remember the causes of clubbing with basal crackles: fibrosing alveolitis, bronchiectasis, asbestosis. Carcinoma should of course always be considered in a clubbed patient with respiratory disease.

Notes

PLEURAL EFFUSION

A common short case. Occasionally needlemarks from diagnostic or therapeutic aspiration are present.

Remember to percuss and auscultate into the axillae. Listen for bronchial breathing and test for aegophony at the upper level of an effusion.

It will not usually be possible to suggest the underlying cause of the effusion although you should look for clues e.g. signs of cardiac failure; clubbing and cachexia (suggesting bronchial carcinoma); rheumatoid hands; butterfly rash of systemic lupus erythematosus.

Revise the causes in terms of transudates and exudates.

Notes

PNEUMONIA

With increasing emphasis on acute cases in the examination you should be prepared to examine patients with (usually resolving) pneumonia. Revise the signs.

Notes

PULMONARY FIBROSIS

Patients with apical fibrosis commonly appear as short cases and you must be able to demonstrate the signs confidently.

The chest may be flattened over an area of fibrosis; this and tracheal deviation towards the affected side are vital clues. Expansion will be reduced on the affected side and the percussion note dull. Remember that low-pitched bronchial breathing may be heard over an area of fibrosis.

Always look carefully for scars: patient may have had one of the operations for tuberculosis performed more commonly in the past: plombage; thoracoplasty; phrenic nerve crush; artificial pneumothorax.

Patients who have had a lobectomy may also be shown.

NB. Although most cases of apical fibrosis are tuberculous in origin, radiotherapy is an important cause to remember (look for markings).

Rarely, ankylosing spondylitis may cause apical fibrosis (see p. 144).

Notes

SUPERIOR VENA CAVAL OBSTRUCTION

A rare 'spot diagnosis' case. You may be asked to observe the patient from the end of the bed. The patient is often tachypnoeic.

You must be able to recognise the characteristic suffused and oedematous appearance of the face, neck and arms; there are dilated and tortuous veins on the anterior chest wall and upper limbs. There is non-pulsatile elevation of the jugular venous pressure. If the obstruction is due to bronchial carcinoma (as is often the case), the markings for radiotherapy may be visible. Much rarer causes include enlargement of the thyroid or thymus glands.

Notes

2.2 THE ABDOMINAL SYSTEM

Scheme of examination of the abdominal system

'Examine the abdominal system'

Action	Notes
Introduce yourself and ask permission to examine patient	
Position patient lying flat on the bed with one pillow. Expose abdomen completely, including inguinal regions but not genitalia.	
Quickly inspect hands for clubbing, leuconychia, Dupuytren's contracture, liver palms, splinter haemorrhages, spider naevi	*These observations should be carried out very quickly as it is usually the abdomen which contains the major abnormality*
Glance at sclerae for jaundice, conjunctivae for anaemia	
Look for spider naevi on the face and chest	
Inspect the tongue	
Palpate cervical and supraclavicular lymph nodes	
Stand at end of bed and observe the abdomen while the patient takes a deep breath	*Look for scars, symmetry, asymmetry, distension, pulsations*
Kneel on the floor or sit on a chair so that you are relaxed and palpate the abdomen	*With a high bed this may not be practicable*

First do a 'scout' palpation for masses or organomegaly. Initially palpate lightly, asking the patient to let you know if there is any tenderness.

NB. large masses, spleens, livers are often visible on inspection, making the rest of the examination much easier

Then palpate again more deeply

If you find a mass, determine its characteristics at this stage

Palpate groin for glands. Check hernial orifices.

Palpate for the liver and percuss out its upper and lower borders

If liver is enlarged, auscultate over it for a bruit

Palpate for a spleen. Remember you must ask the patient to roll onto his right side, if you want to confidently exclude minor splenomegaly.

Palpate for renal enlargement

Percuss for ascites and test for shifting dullness, if this is suspected

Auscultate abdomen for bruits (especially on either side of umbilicus for renal artery stenosis) and bowel sounds

Systolic bruit over liver, hepatocellular carcinoma, hepatoma, alcoholic hepatitis (occasionally), large arteriovenous malformation (rarely)

Tell the examiners that you would normally both examine the genitalia and perform a rectal examination (but never conduct during examination)

Venous hum in region of umbilicus or xiphoid in portal hypertension due to collateral flow

Bruits of renal artery stenosis – lateral to umbilicus or in loins

POPULAR SHORT CASES ON THE ABDOMINAL SYSTEM

ABDOMINAL SHORT CASES

You must be absolutely precise in your method of examination and description of the liver, spleen, kidneys and any abdominal mass.

Watch the patient's face to make sure you do not hurt him during the examination.

HEPATOMEGALY

Always percuss out the upper and lower borders of the liver (the upper border is normally in the fifth intercostal space but may be displaced downwards if the patient has emphysema).

Describe any enlargement in centimetres (easily measured with a pocket ruler) or finger breadths below the costal margin. Comment on the edge, surface, consistency, tenderness, and pulsation.

Auscultate for a bruit over the liver (heard in hepatocellular carcinoma, occasionally alcoholic hepatitis and rarely with a large arteriovenous malformation.). A friction rub may occur with malignant deposits. If the liver is pulsatile look for other signs of tricuspid regurgitation (see p. 52).

Having found hepatomegaly you must proceed with the remainder of the abdominal examination, looking especially for splenomegaly, ascites, and lymphadenopathy – the presence or absence of which alters the differential diagnosis (see hepatosplenomegaly, p. 24).

Remember the possibility of a Riedel's lobe (more common in women) which may extend laterally down as far as the right lumbar region.

You should now spend a few seconds glancing for peripheral clues (see p. 28) in the hands, eyes, (? jaundice, ? xanthelasmata, ? Kayser-Fleischer rings), jugular venous pulse (? elevated – suggests right ventricular failure) and skin (? pigmented as in haemochromatosis or primary biliary cirrhosis; ? scratch marks, ? spider naevi (prominent in primary biliary cirrhosis). Do not spend long doing this, however, as you may waste time and irritate the examiners.

List the causes of hepatomegaly. Remember that common causes include:

- Congestive cardiac failure
- Cirrhosis (but note that liver may become impalpable in advanced cases)
- Carcinomatosis
- Infections (e.g. infective hepatitis, infectious mononucleosis)

Revise the physical features of the liver in each of these cases.

Popular examination cases to remember are haemochromatosis and primary biliary cirrhosis (see p. 30)

Notes

SPLENOMEGALY

A common short case used to test your skills of abdominal examination.

Always start palpation in the right iliac fossa to avoid missing massive splenomegaly. A spleen 'tip' may be better felt with the patient rolled onto his right side with the left arm extended and the left hip and knee flexed.

You will almost invariably be asked to justify your diagnosis in terms of the classical signs:

* Dull to percussion (continuous with area of splenic dullness over 9th, 10th and 11th ribs in midaxillary line)
* Enlarges obliquely towards right lower quadrant
* Distinct edge with medial notch may be palpable
* Downward movement on inspiration
* Cannot palpate above the swelling

You must have an organised list of causes of massive, moderate and slight splenomegaly at your fingertips. A suggested scheme is outlined below but you should expand this or devise your own for ease of memorising. Remember to give the causes common in this country first e.g. myelofibrosis, rather than kala-azar, for massive splenomegaly.

Massive	(>8 cm)	myelofibrosis, chronic myeloid leukaemia, malaria, kala-azar Gaucher's disease.
Moderate	(4–8 cm)	the above plus haemolytic anaemias, lymphoproliferative disease, portal hypertension.
Slight	(4 cm)	all the above plus infections (NB. infectious mononucleosis, infective endocarditis). Blood disorders (e.g. polycythaemia rubra vera, idiopathic thrombocytopenic purpura, pernicious anaemia, systemic lupus erythematosus, sarcoidosis, amyloidosis, Felty's syndrome).

Remember that, as always, if you mention a rare disease, you may be asked to discuss it.

Notes

HEPATOSPLENOMEGALY

A very common short case. As always your technique for demonstrating enlargement of the organs must be quick and accurate. Proceed swiftly to complete your abdominal examination and look carefully for signs of ascites, chronic liver disease and especially generalised lymphadenopathy (examine inguinal, axillary, cervical and supraclavicular regions).

As leukaemias are a common cause of hepatosplenomegaly, test for sternal tenderness if you suspect this diagnosis.

You will be asked the differential diagnosis in your patient: the following is intended as a guide to some common causes. You should expand it yourself as a revision exercise.

LIVER + SPLEEN	Chronic Myeloid Leukaemia usually SPLEEN ++ Myelofibrosis LIVER + Lymphoproliferative disorders – usually SPLEEN+ LIVER+ (superficial nodes may not be palpable even when mediastinal or retroperitoneal nodes are enlarged) NB. Cirrhosis + portal hypertension may exist without ascites but signs of chronic liver disease will be present In a young patient remember β-thalassaemia major: usually LIVER++ SPLEEN++. Look for slate-grey skin (iron deposition) and bossed skull.
LIVER + SPLEEN + NODES	<div align="right">Chronic lymphocytic leukaemia</div> Lymphoproliferative disorders <div align="center">Lymphoma</div> Rarer causes always worth including in your differential diagnosis are: Systemic lupus erythematosus <div align="center">(look for butterfly rash)</div> <div align="center">Sarcoidosis (look for skin lesions)</div>

SPLEEN + LYMPH NODES	As for liver, spleen and nodes but remember Infections ⟨ Acute e.g. infectious mononucleosis Chronic e.g. tuberculosis, brucellosis Felty's syndrome (popular in examinations, look for rheumatoid hands)

ISOLATED
SPLENO-
MEGALY
	Infections e.g. septicaemia
	                infective endocarditis (look for
	                splinter haemorrhages)
	                typhoid
	
	Haematological causes:
	
	Haemolytic anaemia (e.g. Hereditary spherocytosis: anaemia and jaundice present)
	
	Myelofibrosis ⎫
	CML ⎬ spleen may be massive
	
	Lymphoma
	
	Idiopathic thrombocytopenic purpura (anaemia and purpura present)
	
	Polycythaemia rubra vera (plethoric face)
	
	Cirrhosis and portal hypertension: liver may be impalpable but signs of chronic liver disease usually present.

Notes

RENAL ENLARGEMENT

Patients with bilateral renal enlargement are commonly shown in the short cases. The usual cause is polycystic kidney disease: the kidneys may sometimes be grossly enlarged and can even meet in the middle.

Rarer causes include bilateral hydronephrosis and amyloidosis. If you suspect polycystic kidneys you should ask to take the blood pressure (raised in over 50% of cases). Revise the other complications of this condition. Having diagnosed a mass as a kidney you must be able to support this with your physical findings:

* Bimanually palpable
* Ballotable
* Resonant to percussion
* Examining hand can get between swelling and costal margin
* Slight movement downwards on inspiration

Remember that the lower pole of the normal right kidney is often palpable in slim people.

Some patients with polycystic disease of the kidneys also have a polycystic liver which may be palpable. Another association is with berry aneurysms (remember that a posterior communicating artery aneurysm may cause a third nerve palsy; look for this).

Unilateral renal enlargement is less commonly shown (causes include renal cyst, carcinoma, hydronephrosis or hypertrophy of a single functioning kidney).

Notes

ASCITES

Remember the five causes of abdominal distension (fat, fluid, flatus, faeces, fetus – according to rumour the last of these has appeared in the clinical on at least one occasion!). Practise your method of testing for shifting dullness and fluid thrill. Always percuss with the finger on the abdomen parallel to the border of the fluid – you will not be able to locate the limit of the ascites otherwise. In the examination ascites is likely to be found in the context of cirrhosis and portal hypertension or abdominal malignancy. Revise the list of causes of ascites, dividing them into transudates and exudates and be able to discuss the investigation and management of a case.

Notes

CHRONIC LIVER DISEASE

This is a very popular case, with numerous signs to be found.

Peripheral signs should be briefly looked for as they often give an early clue as to the diagnosis. Look carefully at:

The hands: clubbing, leuconychia, palmar erythema (NB. Other causes of palmar erythema include rheumatoid arthritis, pregnancy, chronic leukaemia and thyrotoxicosis), Dupuytren's contracture, spider naevi (more than five is pathological), 'liver flap'.

The face: spider naevi, telangiectasia (paper money skin), jaundice, pigmentation (especially in primary biliary cirrhosis and haemochromatosis) central cyanosis (one-third of patients with decompensated cirrhosis have reduced arterial oxygen saturation due to intrapulmonary shunting through AV fistulae (New Eng. J. Med. 263, 73, 1960), hepatic foetor, bilateral parotid enlargement.

The limbs: ankle oedema, muscle wasting, bruising.

The trunk: loss of axillary, chest and pubic hair, gynaecomastia, excoriations.

Examine the
abdomen: Examine especially for hepatomegaly and signs of portal hypertension: splenomegaly, ascites and prominent periumbilical veins (flow in these collaterals is uniformly away from the umbilicus, unlike the situation in inferior venal caval obstruction where the flow in collateral vessels is uniformly upwards). If the liver is impalpable percuss for contraction of the organ (only present in cirrhosis or fulminant hepatic failure). Auscultate over the umbilicus for a venous hum and over the liver for systolic bruit (which may suggest development of hepatocellular carcinoma).

Remember that signs of 'decompensation' including flapping tremor* of the hands (asterixis) – demonstrate with the wrists dorsiflexed, hepatic foetor, development of encephalopathy (constructional apraxia, e.g. inability to copy the drawing of a 'star', is a useful sign) and jaundice. You should comment on their presence or absence.

*NB. A flapping tremor can also be seen in uraemia, respiratory failure or severe heart failure.

Notes

SPECIAL CASES OF CHRONIC LIVER DISEASE

PRIMARY BILIARY CIRRHOSIS

Consider this in a pigmented patient with prominent excoriations (due to marked pruritus). Look carefully for xanthelasmata and xanthomata over joint, skin folds and sites of trauma (including venepuncture). Finger clubbing is common and should be looked for. The spleen is often palpable (50% of cases).

Remember that steatorrhoea in the condition may lead to easy bruising, osteoporosis and osteomalacia (test for tenderness over the spine).

Important associations of the condition include: rheumatoid arthritis, dermatomyositis, autoimmune thyroiditis, the CREST syndrome (**C**alcinosis, **R**aynaud's phenomenon, o**E**sophageal dysfunction, **S**clerodactyly and **T**elangiectasia), Sjögren's syndrome and renal tubular acidosis.

Notes

HAEMOCHROMATOSIS

The patient is typically a middle-aged male with slate-grey skin pigmentation, maximal in exposed parts, groins, axillae, genitalia and old scars (due to melanin) and a characteristically large and firm liver. The spleen is usually palpable but portal hypertension, ascites and hepatocellular failure are rare. Loss of secondary sexual hair is often prominent.

If you suspect the diagnosis, look for signs of arthropathy (due to pyrophosphate and affecting two-thirds of patients) in the metacarpophalangeal and larger joints.

Tell the examiner that you would like to examine:

- Cardiovascular system (for signs of heart failure)
- Urine for glucose (clinical diabetes in 66% of patients)
- Genitalia (for testicular atrophy)

Notes

CHRONIC ACTIVE HEPATITIS

In this case the patient is usually a young female. Notable features include a Cushingoid appearance, acne, hirsutism, cutaneous striae and vascular spiders. The spleen is usually enlarged, even in the absence of portal hypertension.

Revise the associations.

Notes

ABDOMINAL MASSES

List and revise the causes of masses in each segment of the abdomen.

Any mass which you find must be fully described in terms of site, size, shape, surface, mobility, pulsatility, percussion note and presence or absence of bruit.

Many masses are visible on careful observation of the abdomen – never neglect this vital step. Common sources of difficulty include:

1. Epigastric masses: important causes include gastric carcinoma (check for left supraclavicular nodes (Troisier's sign/Virchow's node) and pancreatic pseudocyst. Two 'catches' are:

    *   Left lobe of liver. Furthermore a post-necrotic nodule in a cirrhotic liver may simulate a gastric mass.
    *   Large rectus muscles: these will seem to enlarge if the patient is asked to sit forwards.

Occasionally large retroperitoneal nodes (in lymphoma) may be palpable in the epigastrium or umbilical region.

2. Suprapubic masses are often missed; always remember to palpate in this area. A most important sign of pelvic masses is that their lower limit is not palpable. As well as the urinary bladder, remember the possibility of an enlarged uterus (e.g. fibroids), or ovarian cyst (frequently palpable in the midline) in female patients.

3. Left and right iliac fossae: masses in the abdomen are not the sole property of the surgeons; you should be able to give a differential diagnosis. The following is an abbreviated list, you will find it useful to expand it yourself to include the rarer causes.

RIGHT ILIAC FOSSA	LEFT ILIAC FOSSA
Carcinoma of caecum Crohn's disease Appendix mass	Carcinoma of colon* Diverticular abscess
Less common	**Less common**
Iliocaecal T.B. Ovarian cyst Pelvic (or transplanted) kidney Iliac lymphadenopathy	Crohn's disease Ovarian cyst Pelvic (or transplanted) kidney Iliac lymphadenopathy

*NB. Normal descending and sigmoid colon is often palpable especially if loaded with faeces.

Notes

RIGHT UPPER QUADRANT MASSES

Masses in this area include hepatic (including Riedel's lobe), renal, and colonic swellings; and occasionally an enlarged gallbladder (revise Courvoisier's law and state this if the patient is jaundiced). It is sometimes difficult to distinguish between these masses and in this case you should state your findings followed by a differential diagnosis. You may be asked how you would investigate the patient: mention simple tests first (e.g. urine testing for blood or protein, faecal occult blood, plain abdominal X-rays followed by ultrasound scan; further tests may include barium enema, liver scan, IVP as appropriate.

Notes

AORTIC ANEURYSM

Remember that the abdominal aorta bifurcates at the level of the umbilicus and may be easily palpable in thin patients.

Always test for expansile pulsation which is present with aortic aneurysm but not if the pulsation is being transmitted.

Auscultate over the swelling, a loud bruit (in the absence of a similar bruit in the heart) supports the diagnosis of aneurysm.

Notes

3. STATION 2 – HISTORY TAKING

The history taking section assesses your ability to gather data from a patient, assimilate the information and discuss the case, including how to solve the specific problems that the patient presents. You are not required to examine the patient.

In the five minute interval before the case you will be presented with written instructions, usually in the form of a letter from the patient's General Practitioner. The letter describes the clinical scenario and gives the task of the consultation.

You may make notes on the case to help prepare for the history taking – rough sheets are provided for this purpose. You should use this opportunity to note important questions which you will ask which are pertinent to the case.

The history taking itself lasts 14 minutes and is carried out in the presence of the examiners. The history is taken from a real patient or a 'surrogate' (who plays the part of a patient); in either case the 'patient' will have been briefed on the responses to make during the history taking. There is one minute for reflection and organising of your thoughts, during which time the patient or surrogate leaves the station. This is followed by a five minute discussion led by the examiners concerning the key points from the history and proposed management of the case.

The examiners are evaluating the following three areas:

1. Data gathering
2. Interpretation and use of information gathered
3. Discussion related to the case

3.1 DATA GATHERING

You must:

* Systematically and logically elicit, evaluate and document the presenting complaints (there are often more than one)
* Perform a review of the systems

The following is a suggested systems review:

Cardiovascular
Dyspnoea – at rest or exertion, how severe
Chest pain
Oedema
Palpitation

Respiratory
Cough – sputum
Dyspnoea
Wheezing

Alimentary
Appetite
Weight with changes
Nausea, vomiting, haematemesis
Dysphagia
Pain
Bowel habit – constipation, diarrhoea, changes
Stool – consistency, blood

Genitourinary
Micturition – incontinence, frequency, nocturia, hesitancy, dysuria, haematuria
Menstruation
Sexual functions

Nervous system
Eyesight
Hearing
Headache
Fits, blackouts, dizziness, funny turns
Gait and unsteadiness
Memory
Speech
Insomnia
Mood

Locomotor system
Pain, stiffness, swelling of joints

- Enquire about past medical history
  - Ask about diabetes, jaundice, rheumatic fever, TB, asthma, hypertension, epilepsy
  - Ask about any operations in the past
- Check family history
  - Ask about any illnesses running in the family. Ask if parents still alive, if not what did they die from?
- Note alcohol and smoking history
- Take a history of treatments – including all current medications. Ask if any allergies.
- Take a social history, including activities of daily living and enquire and follow leads concerning psychological factors which may play a role in the case.

During this part of the interview the examiners will also take note of your communication skills – your ability to respond to the patient's comments verbally and non-verbally – with appropriate eye contact and posture. You must have a balance between open questions ('tell me about this pain') and closed questions ('have you had this pain before?'). You must not rush the patient – though keep in mind that you have only 14 minutes for the history including making a problem list (see below) so you may need to stop loquacious patients from dwelling on one point *ad infinitum* in order to complete the exercise on time.

3.2 INTERPRETATION AND USE OF INFORMATION GATHERED

You will also be assessed on your ability to interpret the information you have gathered. You should go through the summary of the history with the patient and check that the information you have collected is correct.

Next, you must use the information collected to create a **problem list**. You should agree on an action plan with the patient. You should allow the patient the opportunity to ask additional questions.

3.3 DISCUSSION OF THE CASE

If the diagnosis is not clear you will need to give a differential diagnosis.

You need to be able to discuss the implications of the patient's problems including any social impact where appropriate.

You must discuss a strategy for solving the patient's problems, including diagnostic investigations and appropriate treatment plan depending on the results.

3.4 EXAMPLES OF CASES

There is an almost infinite number of cases which may be encountered. However it is quite common for patients with at least two problems to be used as cases. Typical cases illustrating this would be as follows:

A 56-year-old woman presents with intermittent diarrhoea for two years. There are no other symptoms of malignancy. There is a family history of bowel cancer. There is considerable anxiety and family problems emerge in the psychological and social history. The differential diagnosis includes irritable bowel syndrome, and a discussion as to investigation and management follows.

72-year-old man with a three month history of increased exertional chest tightness with increasing shortness of breath. History suggests ischaemic pain. History of Ca. bladder treated with radiotherapy. There is also a history of PR bleeding. The patient had an echocardiogram five years ago, (told v. mild valvular problem). The patient's problems must be listed. The differential diagnosis of the chest pain must be given along with proposed investigation(s). Assuming mild aortic stenosis, management should be discussed.

A 65-year-old lady presents with a history of haemoptysis for the past three weeks. She has a history of cervical dystonia. Investigation of the haemoptysis is the main focus of discussion, while management of the dystonia is also discussed secondarily.

In preparing for the examination you and your colleagues should identify suitable cases such as the above on the wards. Your colleagues should prepare written instructions for the case, and undertake several practice runs in a timed manner (14 minutes for history taking only, one minute for reflection and five minutes for questioning by the 'examiners' – in this case your fellow-candidate or colleague), so that you get used to the situation and format of this station.

4. STATION 3 – THE CARDIOVASCULAR AND NEUROLOGICAL SYSTEMS

4.1 THE CARDIOVASCULAR SYSTEM

SCHEME OF EXAMINATION OF THE CARDIOVASCULAR SYSTEM

Action	Notes
Introduce yourself and ask permission to examine the patient	
Position patient with top half undressed at 45 degrees to horizontal	
Stand at end of bed and observe	*? malar flush* *? tachypnoeic* *? scars (e.g. sternotomy)* *? Marfanoid appearance*
Inspect hands	*? clubbing, ? cyanosis* *? splinter haemorrhages*
Examine radial pulse (see p. 42)	*rate; rhythm*
Check other radial pulse simultaneously	*? absent radial*
In younger patients, check for radiofemoral delay. Lift arm and feel for 'radial knock'.	
Glance at antecubital fossa for catheter scars	
Look at eye	*? anaemic* *? Argyll-Robertson pupil*
Look at tongue	*? central cyanosis*
Palpate carotid pulse	*? abnormal character*

Examine jugular venous pulse
(height from sternal angle and
wave form see p. 44)

Examine apex for position and
character of beat

*check for valvotomy scars at
this point*

Feel for heaves and thrills at apex,
and to left and right of sternum

Listen at apex with bell

*Time the heart sounds by
palpating the patient's right
carotid pulse simultaneously*

Repeat auscultation at apex with
patient in left lateral position

? mid-diastolic murmur

Reposition patient comfortably

Listen with diaphragm at:

* Apex
* Below sternum
* 2nd right intercostal space
* Left sternal edge

Ask patient to sit forward and listen
again with diaphragm at 2nd right
intercostal space and left sternal
edge with breath held in expiration

? early diastolic murmur

Listen at lung bases

Inspect for sacral oedema

Inspect for ankle oedema

Ask examiner whether he wishes you to
examine the peripheral pulses or to
measure the blood pressure

POPULAR SHORT CASES ON THE CARDIOVASCULAR SYSTEM

CARDIOVASCULAR SHORT CASES

This is one area in which you can improve greatly and quickly with practice, and you must repeatedly examine cardiac cases until you are confident in your ability to recognise the common heart valve lesions.

Remember that since many cardiac lesions can be suspected or diagnosed before auscultation, you must concentrate carefully on all the steps prior to this.

Revise the signs which you would expect to find in each of the following cases using the space provided to make your own notes.

'EXAMINE THIS PATIENT'S PULSE'

First check the rate and rhythm at the radial pulse (wear a watch with a second hand). Revise the common causes of sinus tachycardia, sinus bradycardia (NB. Drugs e.g. beta-blockers), atrial fibrillation and complete heart block.

If you suspect complete heart block, look for cannon waves in the jugular venous pulse as well as regular 'a' waves occurring more rapidly than the ventricular rate, and variability of the intensity of the first heart sound; remember that a basal systolic ejection murmur is usually present due to increased stroke volume.

In atrial fibrillation 'a' waves will be absent; again the first heart sound varies in intensity. Assess the rate both at the radial pulse and apex and comment on the pulse deficit.

Next always palpate both radial pulses simultaneously. Absent radial pulse occurs as a short case; common causes include congenital, trauma or surgery (e.g. cardiac catheter, Blalock shunt), systemic embolisation (e.g. mitral stenosis; patient usually in atrial fibrillation).

Elevate the arm and feel for 'knock' of a collapsing pulse against your palm.

Always palpate for radiofemoral delay to avoid missing aortic coarctation.

Always palpate a large artery, e.g. the carotid, to assess the volume and character of the pulse. Remember that the carotids may be visible in aortic regurgitation (Corrigan's sign see p. 49).

Remember to listen over the carotid and femoral arteries for bruits.

Common cases include:

* Collapsing pulse (steep upstroke and downstroke). Seen not only in aortic regurgitation but also in presence of large a-v fistulae (occurring on rare occasions in Paget's disease and patent ductus arteriosus). A large volume (but not collapsing) pulse also occurs in high output states e.g. anaemia, thyrotoxicosis, beri-beri.

* Slow rising, plateau or anacrotic pulse of aortic stenosis

* Bisferiens pulse of combined aortic stenosis and regurgitation

* Occasionally pulsus alternans or paradoxus

Notes

JUGULAR VENOUS PULSE

Always be meticulous in positioning the patient at 45° to the horizontal.

If internal jugular venous pulse is not visible immediately:

1. Check for a low level by

*   Pressing on the liver (ask first if this is tender): remember that hepatojugular reflux may have no patho-physiological significance.

*   Lying patient more horizontally

2. Check for a very high pressure, look at ear lobes (these may move with cardiac cycle) and sit the patient vertical.

Measure the vertical height of jugular venous pulse above the sternal angle; in normal individuals this is not more than 2–4 cm. If the pressure is very high the hand veins may be used as a manometer, as they collapse when the hand is held at the appropriate height above the right atrium.

Identify the two main waves by simultaneously palpating the opposite carotid artery ('a' wave just prior to systole; 'v' wave during systole).

Remember that there is no 'a' wave in atrial fibrillation.

The most likely short cases are:

*   Large 'v' waves (tricuspid regurgitation); palpate for systolic impulse in liver and auscultate for murmur (see p. 52)

*   Large 'a' waves; pulmonary stenosis, pulmonary hypertension or tricuspid stenosis; palpate and auscultate over pulmonary area

*   Cannon waves:

Irregular:	complete heart block, multiple extrasystoles,
Regular:	2:1 atrio-ventricular block.
	nodal rhythm (usually)

A steep y descent occurs with any cause of raised jugular venous pressure, especially constrictive pericarditis (NB. Kussmaul's sign, rise in jugular venous pressure on inspiration).

Superior vena caval obstruction (p. 17) causes nonpulsatile elevation of the jugular venous pressure, not affected by pressure on the neck or abdomen.

Finally, in the case of raised jugular venous pressure check for other signs of congestive cardiac failure: ankle and sacral oedema, tender hepatomegaly, basal crackles or pleural effusions.

Notes

MITRAL STENOSIS

This is an extremely common short case in which you can excel if you are well prepared. Revise the signs of the condition and make notes in the space provided. Remember to exercise the patient to bring out the diastolic murmur if you are suspicious or unsure of it.

As well as making the diagnosis you should always comment on the severity of the stenosis (mild, moderate or severe).

Indicators of severity are:

• Distance from the second heart sound to the opening snap (this reflects left atrial pressure)

• Duration of the diastolic murmur

A guide to severity on auscultation is:

a) Mild stenosis: Diastolic murmur occupies half diastole. Opening snap is late (>100 msecs after A_2).

b) Moderate stenosis: Diastolic murmur almost fills diastole. Opening snap about 80 msecs after A_2.

c) Severe stenosis: Diastolic murmur extends throughout diastole. Early opening snap (<60 msecs after A_2).

NB. None but the very experienced can put a time in milliseconds to the distance between A_2 and opening snap and unless you are very confident about this, it would be unwise to do so.

If possible, you should comment on the pliability of the mitral valve.

Remember that if the valve becomes rigid or calcified, the first sound becomes less loud and the opening snap may disappear.

You should also mention the presence or absence of complications:

• Atrial fibrillation

- Pulmonary hypertension:
  - Palpable and loud P_2
  - Large 'a' waves in the jugular venous pulse (remember that these disappear if the patient is in atrial fibrillation)
  - Left parasternal heave due to associated right ventricular hypertrophy
  - In severe cases there may be an early diastolic murmur at the left sternal edge due to pulmonary regurgitation (Graham Steell murmur)
  - Pulmonary ejection click due to dilated pulmonary artery
- Right ventricular failure (NB. The diastolic murmur may become soft or inaudible)
- Tricuspid regurgitation (common in advanced stenosis, see p. 52)

It is better to comment spontaneously on the severity of stenosis, pliability of the valve and presence of complications than to have this information dragged out of you.

Patients with more than one valvular lesion often appear in the Membership. A particularly common example is aortic regurgitation with mitral stenosis. Here one may be faced with the possibility that an apical mid-diastolic murmur is an Austin-Flint murmur. This sounds exactly like that of mitral stenosis and may even have presystolic accentuation. The first heart sound may sometimes be accentuated and is of no help in differentiation. The opening snap is however of help, being absent in the case of an Austin-Flint murmur. Its presence, therefore, confirms mitral stenosis (although its absence does not exclude this diagnosis as it may disappear when the valve is rigid).

The presence of atrial fibrillation also favours the existence of mitral stenosis. In practice, echocardiography is valuable in distinguishing these two causes of mid-diastolic murmurs.

Notes

MITRAL REGURGITATION/MIXED MITRAL VALVE DISEASE

Revise the causes of this common short case. Remember that in mitral regurgitation (but not stenosis) the apex beat may be displaced downwards and outwards and be thrusting in character; a third heart sound is common (not a feature of stenosis) and there may be a soft mid-diastolic murmur due to rapid left ventricular filling.

Mixed mitral valve disease is also common; the problem many candidates have is to decide which is the dominant lesion. The following is a guide to features which, if present, aid this decision:

Dominant mitral regurgitation:
- Apex beat displaced and thrusting
- Third sound rather than opening snap

Dominant mitral stenosis:
- 'Tapping apex' but not displaced
- Loud dominant mid-diastolic murmur
- Loud first heart sound
- Opening snap rather than third sound
- Evidence of severe pulmonary hypertension

A word of warning: never forget to look carefully for a mitral valvotomy scar during your cardiac examination. Remember that after valvotomy the loud first sound and opening snap remain, but diastolic murmurs are shortened or abolished. Some patients, however, develop a degree of mitral regurgitation, and re-stenosis may occur, so that these patients may have the signs of mixed mitral valve disease.

Notes

AORTIC REGURGITATION

An extremely common short case. Usually the collapsing pulse should make you suspect the diagnosis at the beginning of your examination; this is the value of routinely feeling for a radial 'knock' against your palm with the patient's arm held vertically upwards.

Examine the apex carefully for displacement and thrusting character.

The early diastolic murmur is sometimes difficult to hear: always sit the patient forward with the breath held in expiration and listen at the left sternal edge with the diaphragm.

Remember that an ejection systolic murmur is a common finding and does not necessarily imply the presence of aortic stenosis (see mixed aortic valve disease p. 51). The Austin-Flint murmur should be listened for (see mitral stenosis p. 46). Listen at the lung bases for evidence of left ventricular failure. Always tell the examiners that you would like to check the blood pressure.

Do not start to search for additional signs until you have completed the main cardiac examination. If you have time, you may then look very quickly for:

- Visible carotid pulsation (Corrigan's sign)
- Head bobbing (de Musset's sign)
- Capillary pulsation of nail beds (Quincke's sign)

You can ask the examiner if you may listen over the femoral arteries for:

- Pistol shot sounds synchronous with the pulse (Traube's sign)
- To and fro murmur on light compression with diaphragm, the diastolic component of which is diagnostic of aortic regurgitation (Duroziez's sign)

Glance for evidence of rare causes, e.g. Marfan's syndrome, syphilis (Argyll-Robertson pupil), ankylosing spondylitis, rheumatoid arthritis.

Notes

AORTIC STENOSIS

You must be able to recognise the slow rising pulse of this condition (often with an early notch on the upstroke); it should alert you to its existence at the very beginning of the examination. A palpable thrill may be present in the carotids. Remember that the apex tends to be sustained and heaving but is not usually displaced (except in very severe disease when the left ventricle has dilated); there may be an additional palpable presystolic apical impulse due to atrial systole.

Palpate carefully for a systolic thrill in the second right intercostal space.

Listen carefully to the second heart sound: it may be soft if the valve is heavily calcified; paradoxical splitting may occur. There may be a fourth sound, and an ejection click (in valvar stenosis), the latter disappearing if the valve becomes heavily calcified. The murmur is often heard all over the precordium (unlike that of mitral regurgitation); listen for radiation to the carotids. Remember that occasionally the murmur is heard maximally at the left sternal edge or apex. A degree of aortic regurgitation often coexists, so always listen carefully at the left sternal edge for a diastolic murmur in the usual way. Look also for mitral valve disease (it often coexists if the stenosis is rheumatic in origin; atrial fibrillation may give a clue to this possibility).

Always ask if you may take the patient's blood pressure (check for narrow pulse pressure) but note that a normal or even high pulse pressure or systolic pressure does not exclude the diagnosis. Note also that the murmur may soften in the presence of left ventricular failure. The condition must be distinguished from HOCM (see p. 54) and aortic sclerosis. In the latter condition the pulse is normal in character, as is the apex beat and the second sound; there is no ejection click or systolic thrill and the murmur does not generally radiate to the carotid arteries. However, with the advent of echocardiography, many of these cases are now being found to have mild aortic stenosis.

Revise the complications and management (in general valve replacement if symptoms present and or systolic gradient greater than 50 mmHg). This figure is only a guide and operation may be indicated with a lower gradient if the cardiac output is low.

You may be asked the likely aetiology; remember that in a young or middle aged adult the likely cause is a congenital bicuspid valve which has become calcified; rheumatic heart disease is the next most common cause, while in elderly patients calcification in a tricuspid aortic valve may occur.

Notes

MIXED AORTIC REGURGITATION AND STENOSIS

This is a very common case. Remember that a systolic murmur commonly occurs in aortic regurgitation even when stenosis is slight or absent.

Palpate for a bisferiens pulse (a detectable notch halfway up the upstroke).

The most reliable guide to the dominant lesion is the character of the pulse and the pulse pressure. Always ask if you may take the blood pressure for this reason.

In severe stenosis the pulse is small in volume, the blood pressure normal and the pulse pressure narrow (with occasional exceptions).

In severe regurgitation the pulse is large in volume and collapsing in nature, with a wide pulse pressure.

Notes

TRICUSPID REGURGITATION

You must be able to recognise the prominent systolic 'cv' waves in the jugular venous pulse. Look also for a steep 'y' descent. Palpate the liver for a systolic impulse. Palpate for a left parasternal heave and feel also for a thrill in this area; auscultate for a third sound. The murmur is usually heard best at the lower left sternal edge but is sometimes clearly audible at the apex. Other valve lesions may be present, especially mitral regurgitation and/or stenosis, and these should be listened for carefully.

Mitral regurgitation is sometimes difficult to distinguish. Of great importance in this respect is the increase in intensity of the murmur of tricuspid regurgitation on inspiration, and the presence of systolic venous pulsation. Mitral regurgitation is suggested by radiation of the murmur to the axilla and by left ventricular enlargement.

Listen also for a tricuspid diastolic murmur due to either high flow through the valve or concomitant stenosis.

Look for signs of right-sided heart failure, e.g. hepatic enlargement, ascites and peripheral oedema.

Seek for evidence of rare causes, especially multiple venepuncture sites (main-line drug addiction) and facial telangiectases (carcinoid syndrome). The latter disease may be associated with other right-sided heart lesions (especially pulmonary stenosis), and the patient will usually have a hard, irregular, enlarged liver due to metastases.

Revise the causes of the condition. Remember that it often occurs secondary to right ventricular failure.

Notes

MITRAL VALVE PROLAPSE

This is a popular short case, so listen to as many examples as possible during your practice sessions. You must get used to timing the late systolic murmur and/or mid-systolic click. Remember that with posterior leaflet prolapse the murmur may radiate to the left sternal edge.

In some cases the systolic murmur may be mid- or even pan-systolic; the clicks may be multiple and there may be a systolic 'squeak' or 'honk' at the apex.

Remember that most patients are otherwise normal but check for features of Marfan's syndrome in the fingers and palate. You may be asked to discuss the nature of the condition.

It is worth noting that the effects of manoeuvres may sometimes help in distinguishing between the causes of systolic murmurs: the murmur of mitral valve prolapse is increased by the Valsalva manoeuvre, but decreased by squatting; the reverse effects occur with the manoeuvres in both mitral incompetence and aortic stenosis. See table overleaf. You are not recommended to perform these during the examination – although you may suggest them during discussion of the case if appropriate.

Notes

HYPERTROPHIC OBSTRUCTIVE CARDIOMYOPATHY (HOCM)

This is a rare short case. There is a steeply rising jerky pulse.

There may be a thrusting apex (left ventricular hypertrophy) and left parasternal heave (right ventricular hypertrophy). The murmur is a mid or late systolic ejection murmur, best heard in the left third or fourth intercostal space but occasionally maximal at the apex. An 'a' wave in the jugular venous pulse may be present, as may a fourth heart sound. The pansystolic murmur of associated mitral incompetence may occur.

Differentiation from aortic stenosis may be difficult. In HOCM there is no aortic ejection click and the second heart sound is usually normal. The murmur of HOCM radiates poorly to the carotids.

Certain 'bedside manoeuvres' may assist in the diagnosis (see table below). Again you may suggest these to the examiners during discussion of the case but should not perform them routinely.

Effects of bedside manoeuvres on systolic murmurs:

	HOCM	AS	Mitral Valve Prolapse	Mitral Regurgitation
VALSALVA	↑	↓	↑	↓
SQUATTING	↓	↑	↓	↑

Notes

PULMONARY STENOSIS

This condition is not infrequently shown in the Membership; you must examine patients with it to become familiar with the signs.

Vital clues include the ejection click and mid-systolic murmur loudest on inspiration. Palpate for a thrill in the second left intercostal space, this is commonly present. In severe cases there is a left parasternal heave, the click disappears and the second sound becomes widely split with a soft second (pulmonary) element.

Remember also that the condition, although usually congenital, may be associated with carcinoid syndrome (see tricuspid regurgitation).

Another very rare association is with Kallmann's syndrome (gonadotrophin deficiency secondary to LHRH deficiency with anosmia); other congenital defects may coexist.

Notes

ATRIAL SEPTAL DEFECT

This will usually be of the ostium secundum variety.

The pulse volume may be small and there may be a left parasternal heave due to right ventricular hypertrophy.

You must get used to hearing the wide split second sound, not varying with respiration: practice is the only way to do this. Having heard the split second sound always listen carefully at the second left intercostal space for the common ejection systolic murmur due to high flow through the pulmonary valve. There may also be a tricuspid mid-diastolic flow murmur at the lower left sternal edge which will be louder on inspiration.

In the rare ostium primum variety, murmurs of associated lesions (mitral and/or tricuspid regurgitation) may be present.

Look for evidence of pulmonary hypertension (see Eisenmenger's syndrome p. 58) and revise the complications of the condition.

Notes

VENTRICULAR SEPTAL DEFECT

A fairly common short case. The pulse volume may be small if there is a large left to right shunt. There may be a thrill at the lower left sternal edge and a loud 'tearing' pansystolic murmur maximal at this site. Listen also for a mid-diastolic murmur at the apex due to high flow through the mitral valve.

Look for evidence of complications:

* Pulmonary hypertension, leading eventually to Eisenmenger's syndrome (NB. Pansystolic murmur may soften in this case, see p. 58)

* Biventricular failure

* Endocarditis (look for splinter haemorrhages)

Remember that a small defect may produce a loud murmur (Maladie de Roger).

Notes

EISENMENGER'S SYNDROME

In this case you will usually be presented with a patient who is centrally cyanosed and clubbed and you will be asked to examine the cardiovascular system. The pulse volume will usually be small. Look for signs of pulmonary hypertension and right ventricular hypertrophy on palpation:

- Left parasternal heave
- Palpable pulmonary valve closure (pulmonary diastolic shock)

Auscultate for a loud second sound, right ventricular fourth sound, pulmonary ejection click, and early diastolic murmur of pulmonary regurgitation +/- pansystolic murmur of tricuspid regurgitation.

Attempt to identify the cause of the syndrome (often very difficult):

- In atrial septal defect there will be a fixed split second sound.

- In ventricular septal defect the characteristic pansystolic murmur may become soft or disappear, while the second sound may become single (equal pressure in both ventricles).

- In persistent ductus arteriosus the second sound remains normally split: differential cyanosis is diagnostic. (The venous blood is shunted into the descending aorta so that only the lower limbs become cyanosed i.e. differential cyanosis.)

Notes

COARCTATION OF THE AORTA

An uncommon short case. Remember that the constriction is usually just distal to the origin of the left subclavian artery (near the insertion of the ligamentum arteriosum).

Early clues to the lesion on inspection may be greater development of the upper extremities and thorax than the lower extremities and (sometimes) visible scapular collaterals. Usually, however, the first evidence comes from testing for radiofemoral delay, which should therefore be a routine part of your cardiovascular examination. On occasion the left subclavian artery is involved and there may be asymmetrical radial pulses (see p. 42).

Palpate for a thrusting apex (left ventricular hypertrophy) and listen for the systolic murmur of the coarctation, both anteriorly and posteriorly, over the left upper thorax. Listen also for aortic systolic and (occasionally) diastolic murmurs from an associated bicuspid aortic valve, and listen for murmurs of collaterals over the scapulae. Revise the complications and associations of the condition.

Notes

PERICARDITIS

Occasionally a patient with a pericardial friction rub is shown as a short case, the candidate being asked to 'Examine the precordium'.

Revise the causes of this.

Cardiac tamponade and constrictive pericarditis are most unlikely to occur as short cases though you should revise the signs.

Notes

PROSTHETIC HEART VALVES

Patients with metallic prosthetic aortic or mitral valves are sometimes shown as short cases and you must be able to distinguish between them.

Their characteristic sounds are summarised below. Note that 'pig' valves do not produce these sounds.

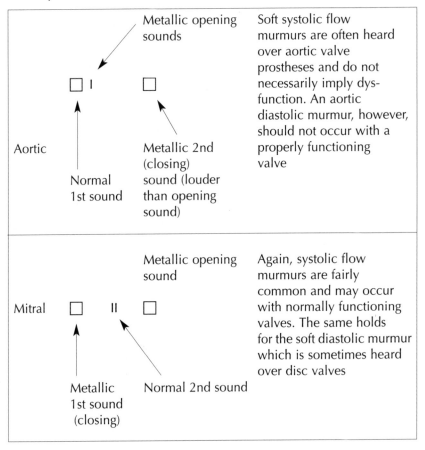

The closing sound is the dominant one with both valves and, by timing this in relation to the carotid pulse, it should be possible to identify rapidly which valve is prosthetic (beware, they may both be!).

Disc valves tend to make a 'clicking' noise on opening or closing while ball and cage valves have a characteristic 'plopping' sound.

Remember that complications of valve replacement include valve leakage or mechanical dysfunction, endocarditis, thromboembolism, bleeding due to anticoagulants and haemolytic anaemia.

Notes

INFECTIVE ENDOCARDITIS

Not common as a short case but always check for splinter haemorrhages*
and clubbing in every cardiovascular examination.

The latter sign implies chronic disease and is less likely to be found in
modern practice.

If you suspect the diagnosis look further at the hands for:

Osler's nodes*
Janeway lesions*

Look for petechial rashes* on the skin and conjunctivae.
Look for the conjunctivae for evidence of anaemia.

Palpate for splenomegaly (40%).

Examine the fundi for Roth's spots*.

Tell the examiner that you would like to test the urine for microscopic
haematuria and/or proteinuria. Say also that you would normally proceed
to examine the chest and limbs for evidence of pulmonary or cerebral
embolism.

Revise the clinical features of the condition (in terms of signs due to):

- Infection
- Embolism
- Immune complex disease
- Cardiac disease

Remember that right-sided lesions (especially tricuspid and pulmonary
regurgitation) occur in main-line drug addicts (look for multiple
venepuncture sites) who usually have no predisposing cardiac lesions.

Remember also that the pattern of the disease is changing with a tendency
for more acute than subacute forms to occur.

*Immune complex phenomena. Glomerulonephritis and neuropsychiatric
manifestations may be due to either emboli or immune complex mediated
vasculitis.

4.2 THE NERVOUS SYSTEM

SCHEME OF EXAMINATION OF NERVOUS SYSTEM

'EXAMINE THE CRANIAL NERVES'

NB. This examination is one in which the candidate who has prepared carefully can readily be distinguished from those who have not.

Practice the 'routine' repeatedly, using this or your own scheme. You should be able to get through it in three or four minutes.

Introduce yourself and ask permission to examine the patient.

I	Ask 'Has there been any change in your sense of smell recently?'
II	Quickly check visual acuity using your pocket reading chart. If the patient wears glasses, he should put them on. Test visual fields with white hat pin. Look for ptosis. Observe pupils and test reaction to light and accommodation. Examine the fundi.
III, IV VI	Test eye movements and observe for nystagmus.
V	Test facial sensation briefly (use cotton wool on both sides). Test corneal reflexes. Test pterygoids 'Open your mouth and don't let me close it'. Test masseters 'Clench your teeth'. Palpate muscles simultaneously. Test jaw jerk.
VII	Test facial muscles:

> 'Smile'
> 'Show me your teeth'
> 'Blow your cheeks out like this'
> 'Raise your eyebrows like this'
> 'Screw your eyes up tightly and don't let me open them'

VIII	Test hearing with a watch. (A watch on a chain is useful for this: digital watches are not.)

'Do you hear my watch ticking? Tell me when the sound disappears'.

Perform Rinne's and Weber's tests (see below).

X	Observe uvula. 'Open your mouth and say aah'.
XI	Test sternocleidomastoids: 'Push your chin against my hand'. Palpate muscles simultaneously.

Test trapezii: 'Shrug your shoulders. Push down simultaneously'.

XII	Look for wasting, fasciculation of the non-protruded tongue.

Look for deviation and weakness: 'Push your tongue out straight. Now move it from side to side.'

Weber's and Rinne's Tests

	CONDUCTIVE DEAFNESS	SENSORINEURAL DEAFNESS
Rinne	BC > AC (negative Rinne)	AC > BC
	IN DEAF EAR	BOTH EARS*
Weber	SOUND REFERRED TO DEAF EAR	SOUND REFERRED TO BETTER EAR
	*False negative Rinne may occur in severe sensorineural deafness: bone conducted sound heard in good ear.	
	BC = bone conduction	AC = air conduction

'EXAMINE THE PATIENT'S UPPER LIMBS'

Action   **Notes**

1. Inspect hands:

    Skin
    Nails
    Joints   (? arthropathy (see p. 142))
    Muscles   (? wasting (see p. 89))
                    (? tremor (see p. 92))

2. Inspect arms:
    Skin (especially elbows). Lesions
    at the elbow common in the short
    cases include:

    Psoriatic plaques
    Rheumatoid nodules
    Xanthomata (see p. 128)
    Gouty tophi (may involve
    olecranon bursa)
    Lesions of pseudoxanthomata
    elasticum (see p. 165)
    Subcutaneous calcification

    Muscles

3. Check pulses bilaterally.

4. Palpate for axillary lymph nodes.

    If the above are negative, proceed to
    neurological examination.

'CARRY OUT A NEUROLOGICAL EXAMINATION OF THIS PATIENT'S UPPER LIMBS'

Introduce yourself and ask the patient's permission to examine his arms. Make sure that the arms are adequately exposed. Look for (and be seen looking for) wasting, fasciculation and scars.

1. **Assess tone:**
   'Let your arm and hand go loose and let me move them for you.'
   (Start at the wrist and move upwards.)

2. **Test power:**
   Start by asking the patient to hold his arms outstretched and then to close his eyes.
   Observe for weakness, parietal drift, or oscillations (see Patten p. 72).

Now proceed rapidly through the muscle groups, starting proximally (as proximal weakness is a common short case):

Action	Notes	
'I'm going to test the strength of some of your muscles.'		
'Hold your arms out to your sides, like this... Now keep them up and don't let me stop you.'	Shoulder abduction: Deltoids	C5
'Now push them in towards you and don't let me stop you.'	Shoulder adduction: Pectorals	C6,7,8
'Pull your arms up towards you and don't let me stop you.'	Arm flexion: Biceps	C5
'Now push me away.'	Arm extension: Triceps	C7
'Clench your fists and bend your wrists up towards you. Don't let me stop you.'	Wrist flexors:	C7
'Now push the other way.'	Wrist extensors:	C7

'Grip my fingers tightly (use two of your fingers).'	Long and short Flexors:	C8,T1
'Put your hand down flat, like this (palm upwards)... and point your thumb towards your nose. Now keep it there and don't let me push it down.'	Thumb abduction: Abductor pollicis brevis; Median nerve	C8,T1
'Spread your fingers wide apart and don't let me push them together.'	Finger abduction: Dorsal interossei; Ulnar nerve	T1
'Now hold this piece of card between your fingers and don't let me pull it away.'	Finger adduction: Palmar interossei; Ulnar nerve	T1

Describe any weakness in terms of the Medical Research Council scale:

Grade	
0	No movement
1	Flicker of movement on voluntary contraction
2	Movement present but not against gravity
3	Movement against gravity but not against resistance
4	Movement against resistance but not full strength
5	Full strength

3. **Test reflexes:**
   Biceps   C5/6
   Supinator   C5/6 If absent, test with reinforcement
   Triceps   C7

4. Test sensation:
(NB. You must be familiar with the anatomical sites of the different dermatomes.)

A Pinprick (use each end of the hat pin)

First demonstrate the stimuli to the patient by testing on the sternum: 'This is sharp... And this is blunt... Now I'm going to test the sensation in your arms and I want you to close your eyes and say 'Sharp' if it feels sharp, and 'Blunt' if it feels blunt.'
Test over each dermatome of each arm quickly.
If sensation to pinprick is impaired, test temperature sensation using a tuning fork (cold) and your hand (warm).

B Light touch

'I want you to say 'Yes' if you feel me touch you with this piece of cotton wool.'

(NB. Do not stroke the skin as this tests tickle, which travels in the spinothalamic tract.)

C Joint position sense

Start with the distal interphalangeal joint of one finger. 'I'm going to move your finger up and down; this is up (move finger up)..., and this is down (move finger down)... Now close your eyes and tell me whether I am moving your finger up or down.' If the patient cannot do this move to more proximal joints progressively.

D Vibration sense

Make the fork vibrate silently (practise this):
'Do you feel this vibrating?' (test on sternum)
'Can you feel it vibrating now?' (test on distal interphalangeal joint of one finger)

If patient cannot feel the vibration, move progressively to more proximal joints.

5. Test coordination:

'Touch my finger with your index finger. Now touch your nose.' (Move patient's hand for him once if he has difficulty in understanding what is required.) 'Now do the same as quickly as possible and keep going.'

Notes

'EXAMINE THIS PATIENT'S LOWER LIMBS'

Here again, you should list the various abnormalities which you might observe at each step of the examination.

Action   **Notes**

Observe:

Skin
NB. Ulcers (see p. 133)
Do not forget soles of feet
and between toes
Lesions on shins (see p. 132)

Joints/bones
NB. Swollen knee joint (see p. 149)
Paget's disease (see p. 158)

Muscles

Calves/ankles (Look carefully for
oedema, see p. 135)

Palpate peripheral pulses and
inguinal nodes. Auscultate over
femoral arteries.

If the above are negative,
proceed to neurological
examination

'CARRY OUT A NEUROLOGICAL EXAMINATION OF THIS PATIENT'S LOWER LIMBS'

Introduce yourself and ask permission to examine the patient. Ensure that the legs are fully exposed but also make sure that the patient remains 'decent'. Observe for wasting and fasciculation.

1. Assess tone:

    'Let your leg go loose and let me move it for you'. Use more than one method: roll the leg from the knee, then with a hand behind the knee, flex the leg and feel for any 'catch'. Then passively flex the leg at the knee and hip joints. If tone is increased, test for knee and ankle clonus.

2. Test power (start proximally):

'I'm going to test the strength of some of the muscles in your legs. Keep your leg straight and lift it up into the air. Now keep it up and don't let me stop you.'	Hip flexion: Iliopsoas	L1,2
'Now push your leg down into the bed and don't let me stop you.'	Hip extension Glutei	L4,5
'Push out against my hand.'	Hip abduction Glutei	L4,5
'Push in against my hand.'	Hip adduction: Adductor group	L2,3,4
'Bend your knee and pull your heel up towards you: don't let me stop you.' (Hold ankle.)	Knee flexion Hamstrings	L5,S1
'Now straighten your knee out.'	Knee extension: Quadriceps	L3,4

'Pull your foot up to you and don't let me stop you.'	Ankle dorsiflexion: Tibialis anterior and long extensors L4,5
'Push your foot down against my hand.'	Ankle plantar flexion: Gastrocnemius S1
'Push your foot out against my hand.'	Eversion of foot: Peronei S1
'Push your foot in against my hand.'	Inversion of foot Tibialis anterior L4 and posterior

Any weakness should be described in terms of the Medical Research Council scale.

3. Test reflexes:

    Knee L4
    Ankle S1   If absent, test with reinforcement.

4. Test plantar responses: use an 'orange stick' (see Patten p.141).

5. Test sensation:

    Pinprick, light touch, vibration sense and joint position sense as described for the upper limbs. When testing joint position sense remember to hold the lateral aspect of the big toe (see Patten p.174).

6. Test coordination:

    Use the heel-shin test.

7. Perform Romberg's test

    Tell the examiners that you would like to examine the patient's gait.

NEUROLOGICAL SHORT CASES

The examination of neurological short cases requires a great deal of polish and confidence which can only be achieved through practice. It is certainly a great advantage to have done a neurology job and if you have not done so, it might be worth considering attending one of the special courses on neurology for the Membership. In any case, you must devote plenty of time to neurological cases during your practice sessions.

Visual field defects

Revise the causes of the following field defects which occasionally appear as short cases:

	NOTES
Homonymous hemianopia	
Bitemporal hemianopia	
Central scotoma	
Concentric constriction	

Remember that a homonymous hemianopia, the commonest case, implies a lesion posterior to the optic chiasm (in the optic tract, radiation or occipital cortex). Note the following:

- A lesion in the anterior occipital cortex (e.g. due to posterior cerebral artery occlusion) causes a macular sparing hemianopia; (see Patten p.19)

- Lesions in the optic tract may lead to an incongruous hemianopia

- Lesions of the optic radiation may produce an upper quadrantic hemianopia with a temporal lobe lesion, or a lower quadrantic hemianopia with a parietal lobe lesion.

PUPILLARY ABNORMALITIES

HORNER'S SYNDROME

This is a very common short case. 'Look at this man's eyes'.

- The ptosis and meiosis should be readily apparent. Check for the other features: enophthalmos and loss of forehead sweating on the same side. In congenital cases the iris remains blue/grey; look for this.

- Test the reactions to light and accommodation, these should be present and normal.

- Proceed to inspect the neck for scars from cervical sympathectomy (a common short case) or thyroidectomy.

- Palpate for cervical rib and cervical lymphadenopathy.

- Examine for weakness of the small muscles of the hand (T1) and for loss of sensation over the T1 dermatome (T1 involvement, commonly due to Pancoast's syndrome).

- Test for loss of pain and temperature in the arm and face, loss of arm reflexes, bulbar palsy and nystagmus (syringomyelia/syringobulbia).

- Tell the examiner that you would like to examine the chest clinically and radiologically for evidence of Pancoast's tumour.

- Revise the list of causes of the syndrome according to their anatomical level:

i.e. Hemisphere, Brain stem, Cervical cord, T1 root, Sympathetic chain.

Notes

HOLMES-ADIE (MYOTONIC) PUPIL

The patient is often a healthy young female; the unilateral dilated pupil is striking. The eye is in the normal position with no ptosis.

- Look for ptosis and test ocular movements for evidence of third nerve palsy (the main alternative diagnosis)
- Test the response to light (very slow) and accommodation (also slow but more definite)
- Ask the examiner's permission to test the knee jerks (often absent)

Remember that the Holmes-Adie pupil constricts promptly to 2.5% methacholine. However a word of warning: another cause of unilateral dilated pupil (usually fixed to light and accommodation) is mydriatic eye drops!

Notes

ARGYLL ROBERTSON PUPILS

The pupils are small and irregular and react to accommodation but not to light.

The commonest cause is tabes dorsalis.

Look for associated signs of tabes including wrinkled forehead with ptosis, absent ankle jerks, loss of joint position sense and vibration sense, positive Romberg's test and sensory ataxia, Charcot's knee joint and aortic insufficiency...

Note that the condition, thought to be due to a lesion in the tectum of the midbrain, may also occur occasionally in diabetes mellitus.

Notes

AFFERENT PUPILLARY DEFECT

This defect may be caused by lesions of the retina (including severe macular degeneration), optic nerve, chiasm and optic tract. It is particularly associated with optic nerve damage in multiple sclerosis. The pupillary response is also known as a Marcus-Gunn pupil (Patten p. 8). When the normal eye is stimulated by a bright light, the pupil constricts and remains constricted. In contrast, the pupil of the affected eye reacts slowly, less completely and transiently, so that it may start to dilate again even while the light is still shining on it – the so-called pupillary escape phenomenon. This reaction is best seen if the light is rapidly alternated from one eye to the other, each stimulus lasting 2–3 seconds, with a second between. While the normal pupil constricts and stays small, the abnormal pupil dilates instead of constricting as the light falls on it – the so-called **swinging light test**.

Notes

OCULAR PALSIES

These are commonly shown ('Examine these eyes' or 'This man has double vision, would you examine his eyes').

On inspection III and VI nerve palsies may be obvious. You must quickly demonstrate which muscles are weak and the direction in which reported diplopia is maximal. In less obvious cases you should be able to analyse the diplopia by using the cover test (when looking in the direction of action of the weak muscle, the outer image disappears on covering the affected eye).

In the case of a III nerve palsy you must state whether the lesion is complete or partial. In a complete lesion there is complete ptosis, the eye is deviated downwards and outwards with loss of upward, downward and medial movements, and a dilated, unreactive pupil. It is obviously necessary to elevate the eyelid to observe the latter findings because of the ptosis. Note that in vascular lesions of the III nerve (e.g. in diabetes, arteriosclerosis or arteritis) the pupil may be spared.

You should demonstrate whether the IV nerve is intact by lifting the eyelid and asking the patient to look down: if the nerve is intact there will be intorsion of the eye (see Patten p.50). Test lateral gaze to confirm that the VI nerve is intact.

You may be asked the likely cause: remember that the commonest causes of a pure III nerve palsy are posterior communicating artery aneurysm, diabetes, atherosclerosis, and raised intracranial pressure. The latter three are also common causes of a VI nerve palsy.

Revise the full list of causes of ocular palsies, dividing them into lesions in the brain stem, base of skull, cavernous sinus and orbit.

Remember that the III, IV and VI nerves may be affected singly or in combination as part of a cranial neuropathy due to:

*   Diabetes
*   Polyarteritis nodosa
*   Multiple sclerosis
*   Sarcoidosis
*   Basal meningitis: tuberculous, syphilitic, carcinomatous

There are two traps to be wary of:

1. Congenital squint: the eyes move together, the angle between their longitudinal axis remaining constant.

2. Dysthyroid eye disease and myasthenia gravis: both may produce complex eye signs due to involvement of the eye muscles. Always look for exophthalmos, a goitre or thyroid scar, or (in myasthenia) bilateral ptosis.

There is an excellent illustrated account of ocular palsies in *Diagnosis in Color, Neurology,* Parsons, M and Johnson, M, Mosby/Harcourt Health Sciences, 2001.

Notes

NYSTAGMUS

You will usually be asked to 'Examine these eyes' and you must always look carefully for nystagmus, both on horizontal and on vertical gaze (candidates often miss the latter through failing to observe specifically for it). Remember to keep within the range of binocular vision and wait for at least five seconds in each position. Describe the nystagmus in terms of its type, direction of fast phase and maximal amplitude. Note that in vestibular nystagmus the fast phase is away from the side of the lesion, while in cerebellar nystagmus the opposite is true. Brain stem nystagmus is typically multidirectional, and may be vertical or rotary.

Remember that pendular nystagmus (a rare short case: look for pink eyes of albinism) is associated with poor visual acuity.

Some neurologists also grade nystagmus into:

Grade 1:   Present on looking in one direction only.
Grade 2:   Present with the eyes in the neutral position.
Grade 3:   Present on looking to either side.

Be able to give the common causes of nystagmus.

Ataxic nystagmus is a popular case so be sure that you can demonstrate the signs (nystagmus greater in abducting eye often with associated weakness of adduction due to internuclear ophthalmoplegia).
NB. The lesion is in the median longitudinal bundle and strongly suggests multiple sclerosis.

When you have completed your examination of the eyes (remember to check for optic atrophy, which is often present if the patient has multiple sclerosis), you may ask permission to look for signs elsewhere to elucidate the cause. In particular, it may be helpful to test for cerebellar signs (e.g. finger-nose test), test the hearing (e.g. Ménière's disease) and inspect the tympanic membrane for evidence of otitis media.

Notes

FACIAL NERVE PALSY

You must be able to distinguish between upper and lower motor neurone lesions of the VII nerve, as well as having lists of their causes ready.

You must be able to demonstrate the global unilateral facial weakness present after a lower motor neurone lesion (a common case, usually due to Bell's palsy). Have a series of commands ready, for example: 'raise your eyebrows like this', 'wrinkle your forehead like this', 'smile', 'show me your teeth', 'whistle'.

- Palpate for parotid enlargement (the VII nerve may be involved in malignant tumour)

- Inspect the external auditory meatus and fauces for vesicles (Ramsay-Hunt syndrome) and the tympanic membrane for evidence of otitis media (a rare cause today)

- Tell the examiner that you would like to ask the patient whether he has become intolerant to high-pitched or loud sounds (hyperacusis due to paralysis of stapaedius muscle) and that you would normally test taste sensation on the anterior two-thirds of the tongue (involvement of chorda tympani).

In a patient with bilateral lower motor neurone facial weakness consider Guillain-Barré syndrome and sarcoidosis (bilateral Bell's palsy is very rare).

Notes

PERIPHERAL NEUROPATHY

This is a common short case: you should be able to demonstrate the symmetrical peripheral diminution of sensation to all modalities +/- motor weakness. Diminution or absence of reflexes is a most important finding: always test again with reinforcement.

- Look for trophic changes and Charcot's joints. Common causes of the latter are diabetes mellitus, syringomyelia (especially shoulder joint).

- Palpate for tenderness of affected muscles which is common in diabetic or alcoholic polyneuropathy. Palpate for thickened peripheral nerves present in:

  - Amyloidosis
  - Refsum's disease (cerebellar damage, peripheral neuropathy, deafness and retinitis pigmentosa)
  - Leprosy
  - Dejerine-Sottas disease (hypertrophic peripheral neuropathy)
  - Charcot-Marie-Tooth disease (peroneal muscular atrophy) some thickening detectable in 25% of cases. (See Patten p.xxx)

- Glance briefly for clues as to the cause:

  - Insulin injection sites (diabetes mellitus)
  - Signs of chronic liver disease (especially alcoholic)
  - Anaemia and slight jaundice (B12 deficiency, but note that neuropathy may occur without haematological disturbance)
  - Cachexia (malignancy)
  - Pigmentation, anaemia and brown line on nails +/- evidence of haemodialysis (uraemia)
  - Pes vacus (peroneal muscular atrophy or Friedreich's ataxia)
  - Rheumatoid hands, or butterfly rash of systemic lupus erythematosus

Remember that a predominantly motor neuropathy occurs in:

- Guillain-Barré syndrome
- Peroneal muscular atrophy
- Lead poisoning
- Porphyria

A predominantly sensory neuropathy often occurs in:

- Diabetes mellitus
- Malignancy (especially Ca bronchus)
- Vitamin B12 and B1 deficiency
- Chronic renal failure
- Leprosy

Remember that the combination of peripheral neuropathy with cranial nerve involvement may occur in diabetes mellitus, sarcoidosis, Guillain-Barré syndrome (especially bilateral LMN VII palsy) and polyarteritis.

Revise the causes of mononeuritis multiplex.

The ulnar, median and radial peripheral nerve lesions are occasionally shown as short cases: make notes on the signs which you would look for with lesions at different levels of the following (see Patten p. 293).

Notes

ULNAR NERVE LESION

Usually due to lesion at the elbow; inspect for scars or arthritis.

Occasionally due to repeated trauma to heel of hand (no sensory loss in this case).

Notes

MEDIAN NERVE LESION

Carpal tunnel syndrome is a common case.
NB. Associations include pregnancy, myxoedema, rheumatoid arthritis, acromegaly, trauma.

Remember that sensory loss is very variable and that the palm is spared since the palmar branch of the medial nerve passes superficial to the flexor retinaculum.

Notes

RADIAL NERVE LESION

Notes

a) Axilla

b) Spiral groove
    (spares triceps and
    triceps reflex)

c) Posterior interosseous
    nerve

Notes

UNILATERAL FOOT-DROP

Here the main differential diagnosis is between:

- Pyramidal lesion affecting lower limb (e.g. cerebrovascular accident; multiple sclerosis: pyramidal weakness, hyperreflexia and upgoing plantar should make diagnosis obvious).

- Common peroneal nerve palsy; weakness of dorsiflexion of feet and toes and of eversion of foot. Ankle jerk is intact and plantar response normal; sensory loss often restricted to dorsum of foot (may extend to anterolateral aspect of leg below knee).

- L5 lesion often due to prolapsed intervertebral disc. Weakness of dorsiflexion but not eversion of foot (latter supplied by S1). Ankle jerk is intact, plantar response normal, sensory loss on dorsum of foot often extending to lateral aspect of leg below knee.

Notes

SPASTIC PARAPARESIS

A common case. You will be asked to examine the legs. You must be able to show the signs with style and polish. Never forget to test for a sensory level and for absence of the abdominal reflexes. Tell the examiners that you would normally ask the patient about bowel and bladder function and test sacral sensation.

If allowed to proceed, you should examine the arms. You may be able to localize the lesion (NB. C5/6, absent biceps/supinator jerks, brisk triceps jerk). Ask the examiner's permission to test the neck movements. Again, be ready with your differential diagnosis, which as well as cord compression should include multiple sclerosis, transverse myelitis, subacute combined degeneration of the cord (peripheral neuropathy usually present), anterior spinal artery thrombosis (dorsal columns spared) and parasagittal meningioma.

Notes

WASTING OF THE SMALL MUSCLES OF THE HAND

A popular case ('Examine these hands').

Remember that rheumatoid arthritis and old age are common causes of this. First establish whether the wasting and weakness is generalised or whether it is restricted to the muscles supplied by the median or ulnar nerves (test abductor pollicis brevis and interossei). NB. Combined median and ulnar nerve lesions will of course produce generalised weakness and wasting but this is rare; distal muscular atrophy is another rare peripheral cause.

If the disturbance is generalised the lesion is likely to be central: i.e.

- Lesions of the cord affecting T1
  e.g.   Motor neurone disease
                  Syringomyelia

- Lesions affecting T1 Root
  e.g.   Neurofibroma
                  Cervical spondylosis (relatively rare at this level)

- Lesions of the brachial plexus affecting T1
  e.g.   Klumpke's paralysis
                  Cervical ribs
                  Pancoast tumour

Your should therefore

- Look for fasciculation in the hand and arm (prominent in motor neurone disease: if you suspect this diagnosis proceed as on p. 99) and look for wasting and weakness in the rest of the arm.

- Test for loss of reflexes and spinothalamic sensation in the arm (syringomyelia)

- Test sensation over T1 dermatome

- Palpate for cervical ribs

- Observe for Horner's syndrome (see p. 75)

PROXIMAL MYOPATHY

The candidate is usually asked to examine the lower limbs neurologically.

Remember the common causes:

- Polymyositis/dermatomyositis (NB. Tender muscles, rashes, especially on cheeks, eyelids (heliotrope), and over small joints of hands)

- Cushing's syndrome (ask about history of steroid ingestion)

- Thyrotoxicosis (look for goitre, eye signs, rapid pulse, tremor)

- Carcinoma

- Diabetes (amyotrophy: asymmetrical especially in lower limbs of middle-aged or elderly male non-insulin dependent diabetics)

- Osteomalacia

- Hereditary muscular dystrophy

Notes

CEREBELLAR SIGNS

Occasionally you will simply be asked to 'Demonstrate some cerebellar signs on this patient'. Cerebellar testing may also come up in the context of ataxia or tremor and you must be able to go through a range of tests:

Look for:

- Intention tremor/past-pointing (dysmetria) in finger-nose test

- Oscillation of upper limb in outstretched arm test

- Dysdiadochokinesia on rapid supination/pronation if wrist and hand-tapping

- Lower limb ataxia with heel-shin test

- Hypotonia, pendular reflexes

- Nystagmus

- Scanning dysarthria

- Ataxic gait (falls towards affected side) or truncal ataxia

Revise the causes of cerebellar signs: demyelinating disease is common and should be mentioned early

Notes

TREMOR

You may be asked to look at the hands or to 'Examine the arms neurologically'. Having found a tremor, you must determine whether it is of resting, postural or intention type. Always test the tone in the arms carefully as this may reveal extrapyramidal rigidity. With postural tremor you should look for signs of thyroid disease and tell the examiner that you would like to know whether there is a family history of tremor and whether the patient is on any medications (e.g. salbutamol, lithium). With an intention tremor, test for other cerebellar signs (see p. 91).

Notes

OTHER DYSKINESIAS

Revise the definitions and causes of chorea, athetosis, dystonia, hemiballismus, myoclonus and tics. Chorea is sometimes shown: remember that drugs (e.g. neuroleptics, L-dopa) are a common cause. 'Senile' chorea is a cause in the elderly. Tell the examiner that you would like to know if there was a family history of the condition (Huntington's chorea or hereditary non-progressive chorea) and that you would like to test the patient's higher cerebral functions (dementia in Huntington's chorea). Ask about previous rheumatic fever and history or oral contraception.

Rare causes worth remembering are polycythaemia rubra vera, thyrotoxicosis and systemic lupus erythematosus.

In younger patients with dyskinesias always check for Kayser-Fleischer rings.

Notes

DYSPHASIA/DYSARTHRIA

The candidate is asked to 'Test this patient's speech', or 'Ask this patient a few questions'.

Start by asking simple questions, such as 'What is your name?', 'Where do you live?'. You should be able to quickly distinguish between disorders of phonation (dysphonia), articulation (dysarthria, see p. 94) and speech content (dysphasia). The latter is the most common short case.

The essential point is to distinguish between expressive and receptive dysphasia. In expressive (Broca's) aphasia the patient has great difficulty in finding the words with which to reply to your questions. In contrast, if the patient has a sensory aphasia, he will reply fluently to your questions but the speech is often irrelevant or unintelligible with jargon, paraphrasias and neologisms.

Test the patient's ability to name objects (wrist watch, second hand and winder on watch). Difficulty in naming objects is found in both motor and sensory aphasia but is relatively selectively impaired in the rare nominal dysphasia (lesion in angular gyrus).

You must now test for comprehension difficulty (pointing towards sensory aphasia) by asking the patient to perform specific tasks e.g. 'Touch your nose', 'Pick up the pen'.

Ask if you may test for alexia and agraphia (indicating extension of damage to parieto-occipital region. NB. May be part of Gerstmann's syndrome, see p. 104).

Remember that many patients have features of both sensory and expressive dysphasia.

You may be asked the site of the lesion:

- Broca's area; inferior frontal gyrus of dominant hemisphere.

- Wernicke's area; posterior part of superior temporal gyrus plus adjacent parts of parietal and occipital cortex of dominant hemisphere.

DYSARTHRIA

Have a selection of tongue-twisters ready to use:

> e.g.   The Methodist Episcopal Church
> Baby hippopotamus
> West Register Street

You must be able to recognise the following types of speech:

* Pseudobulbar (monotonous, high-pitched, indistinct 'hot potato' speech). NB. Emotional liability and bilateral (though often asymmetrical) pyramidal signs are present in pseudobulbar palsy.

* Bulbar (nasal)

* Cerebellar (scanning or staccato)

* Parkinsonian (slow, slurred, low-pitched, monotonous and quiet)

Remember that poorly-fitting or absent, dentures are a common cause of dysarthria; it may also occur with VII nerve palsy (e.g. Bell's palsy).

Notes

HIGHER CORTICAL FUNCTION

Be able to conduct a Mini-Mental State Examination to examine higher cortical function including memory and orientation.

Notes

GAIT

Be able to recognise the gaits listed below and make notes on the signs and causes of each. A popular case is to present the candidate with an ataxic patient: 'Watch this patient walk and then examine anything you think relevant'. It is important that, as well as testing for cerebellar signs, you remember to perform Romberg's test and to check joint position sense and vibration sense to distinguish sensory from cerebellar ataxia. Parkinsonian gait is not to be confused with the short shuffling steps of 'marche au petit pas' occurring in diffuse cerebrovascular disease.

Fill in the signs and causes   Notes

Hemiplegic

Paraplegic

Parkinsonism

Sensory ataxia

Cerebellar

Proximal muscle
weakness (waddling gait)

Notes

PARKINSONISM

This may be presented by asking you to observe the face, to watch the patient walking or to examine the arms neurologically.

Mild cog-wheel rigidity may be reinforced by asking the patient to flex and extend one arm while you are testing tone on the other (sinkinesis).

Bradykinesia may be elicited by asking the patient to touch his thumb with each of his fingers.

The coarse, pill-rolling tremor (4–6 cps) at rest is characteristic.

Pay careful attention to the patient's gait: note that loss of arm swing is an early feature. Look for flexed posture.

Remember to test for a positive 'glabellar tap'. Look for seborrhoea and excessive sweating and test for dysarthria.

Perform a functional test e.g. ask the patient to undo a button.

If there is time you could add an examination for vertical gaze palsy (Steele-Richardson syndrome) and postural hypotension (marked in Shy-Drager syndrome, but may be iatrogenic e.g. L-dopa treatment).

Notes

FRIEDREICH'S ATAXIA
(Autosomal recessive)

Pes cavus may again serve as a clue. The patient will have evidence of cerebellar disturbance (see p. 91) often with concurrent evidence of pyramidal weakness in the legs and impairment of dorsal column-mediated sensation. The ankle jerks disappear before the knee jerks: the condition is one of the causes of absent ankle jerks with extensor plantars (see below).

Look for evidence of heart failure (cardiomyopathy) and optic atrophy.

Causes of absent knee jerks with extensor plantars:

* Motor neurone disease
* Diabetes mellitus
* Subacute combined degeneration of the cord
* Neurosyphilis (tabo paresis)
* Friedreich's ataxia
* Conus medullaris lesion

Remember that a more common cause of mixed cerebellar, pyramidal and dorsal column sign is multiple sclerosis.

Notes

PERONEAL MUSCULAR ATROPHY
(Charcot-Marie-Tooth disease, autosomal dominant)

Suspect this diagnosis in a patient with pes cavus (also seen in Friedreich's ataxia) and wasting of the peronei, and calf muscles and distal third of the thigh (inverted champagne bottle appearance).

Remember that in contrast to motor neurone disease there is usually evidence of mild sensory loss and absent reflexes and plantar responses in the legs (reflexes in the legs are usually brisk in motor neurone disease).

Note that two major forms of the disease are now recognised:

Type I: Hypertrophic type, with enlarged peripheral nerves and segmental demyelination

Type II: Neuronal type, no hypertrophic changes; axonal degeneration

Notes

MOTOR NEURONE DISEASE

A very common short case: the candidate is asked to examine either the upper or lower limbs or (occasionally) the cranial nerves/patient's speech.

The importance of inspection of limbs is great in this case, fasciculation being missed by candidates moving too hastily to the rest of the examination. It may be brought out by flicking the muscles: do this if you are suspicious of fasciculation. NB. Fibrillation is an EMG finding – a common question.

- Remember that there is often a mixture of upper and lower motor neurone signs: commonly the signs in the arms are predominantly of the lower motor neurone type, with mainly upper motor neurone signs in the legs; knee jerks are usually exaggerated.

- Demonstrate absence of sensory loss and ask to look at the patient's tongue (for fasciculation)

- Test the jaw jerk (often exaggerated) and listen to the patient's speech

- If allowed to ask questions, ask about difficulty in swallowing

- Revise the signs of the three classical forms of presentation (amyotrophic lateral sclerosis, progressive muscular atrophy, progressive bulbar palsy) but remember that these are often present together in the same patient. Note also that progressive bulbar palsy is often combined with upper motor neurone signs (e.g. brisk jaw jerk) and evidence of pseudobulbar palsy.

Notes

SYRINGOMYELIA

The candidate is often asked to examine the arms. The classical signs will only be brought out if your method of examination is accurate and thorough. The following refers to a classical case.

* There is wasting of the upper limbs (including the small hand muscles)

* Tone is reduced in the upper limb, as is power, especially distally

* The reflexes in the arms are reduced or absent

* Sensory testing will reveal loss of pain and temperature with preservation of vibration, light touch and joint position sense. These signs are usually asymmetrical (maximal on the same side as the lesion).

Look for evidence of Charcot's joint at the shoulder, which may occur in long-standing cases, and trophic changes in the hands.

Ask the examiner if you may examine the lower limbs (usually pyramidal signs on the side of the lesion). Look for Horner's syndrome and ask whether you may examine the cranial nerves for signs of syringobulbia: loss of pain and temperature sensation on the face (classically progressing forward from behind; sensory loss of the so-called 'onion skin' type); bulbar palsy; nystagmus.

Notes

TABES DORSALIS

Patients with neurosyphilis still appear in the examination. Know the signs of this and of 'general paralysis of the insane' just in case.

Notes

DYSTROPHIA MYOTONICA

A very popular Membership case. The candidate is usually asked to examine the cranial nerves. You must be able to recognise the facial appearance early (see Parsons and Johnson, p.332).

NB.

- Frontal baldness (females may wear a wig)

- Expressionless face and smooth forehead despite ptosis. NB. In tabes dorsalis there is a bilateral ptosis with overactive frontalis muscle.

- Wasting of temporalis and masseters (producing 'hatchet' face) and sternomastoids

- Bilateral ptosis and facial muscle weakness

- Cataracts

Test for the myotonic hand shake. Ask if you may:

- Test limb muscles for weakness and wasting (especially distally)

- Observe for gynaecomastia and testicular atrophy

- Test higher intellectual function (IQ often low and dementia may occur).

Other abnormalities that may occur are diabetes mellitus, cardio-myopathy, respiratory infections (muscular difficulties and IgG deficiency) and disordered oesophageal and bowel motility.

Notes

MUSCULAR DYSTROPHY

Revise the appearance, inheritance and prognosis of the following types (see Patten pp. 315–320) and expand the following chart:

TYPE	FEATURES	IQ	PROGNOSIS
SEVERE X-LINKED. DUCHENNE MUSCULAR DYSTROPHY (uncommon as a short case).	Presents 3rd year of life severe proximal weakness of lower limbs Calf hypertrophy Ankle jerks preserved Cardiac muscles affected Onset 5th–25th year	May be low	Death towards end of second decade
BENIGN X-LINKED. BECKER TYPE MUSCULAR DYSTROPHY.	Weakness and wasting of pelvic and shoulder-girdle muscles	Normal	Many survive to normal age
FACIO SCAPULO-HUMERAL DYSTROPHY (Autosomal dominant).	Onset often in adolescence Facial weakness: ptosis Difficulty in closing eyes Wasting of sternomastoids spinati pectorals triceps biceps Marked scapular winging Occasionally deltoids hypertrophy	Normal	Normal life span
LIMB GIRDLE MUSCULAR DYSTROPHY (Autosomal recessive).	Onset usually in second or third decade Weakness and wasting may begin in either shoulder or pelvic girdle muscles Hypertrophy of calves and/or deltoids may occur Ankle jerks preserved	Normal	Often severely disabled by middle life with death before normal age

NB. A scapuloperoneal muscular dystrophy may occur, which may be a myopathy, a neuropathy, a form of spinal atrophy or a combination of these.

Notes

STROKE

Patients with straightforward strokes are sometimes shown as short cases. The candidate may be asked to 'Assess this patient who has had a stroke', or to 'Examine the limbs'. You should be able to demonstrate the signs quickly and efficiently.

Notes

HEMIPLEGIA

Having elicited the signs in the limbs, test for sensory inattention, visual inattention and hemianopia, and ask if you may test the patient's speech. Show that you are considering the aetiology by feeling the patient's pulse (? atrial fibrillation), auscultating for valve lesions and carotid bruits and taking the patient's blood pressure.

Revise the signs of parietal lobe dysfunction as these are occasionally asked (see p. 104).

Notes

PARIETAL LOBE SIGNS

1. Either hemisphere

- Loss of accurate localisation of touch, joint position sense and temperature appreciation (see Patten p.73). NB. Parietal drift in outstretched arm test.

- Loss of two-point discrimination

- Astereognosis

- Dysgraphaesthesia

- Sensory inattention

- Sometimes: attention hemianopia, homonymous hemianopia or lower quadrantic hemianopia

2. Dominant parietal lobe

Additional features

- Receptive dysphasia
- Gerstmann's syndrome (if lesion in angular gyrus):
    - Dysgraphia and dyslexia
    - Dyscalculia
    - Left-right disorientation
    - Finger agnosia
    - Ideomotor apraxia may be associated
- Bilateral ideomotor apraxia (unable to imitate gestures)
- Bilateral ideational apraxia (failure to execute composite actions e.g. lighting a match when given a closed box)

3. Non-dominant parietal lobe

- Dressing apraxia
- Constructional apraxia
- Hemiasomatognosia (loss of appreciation of opposite side of body) or neglect of opposite side

Notes

LATERAL MEDULLARY SYNDROME

Revise the signs of this syndrome (due to posterior inferior cerebellar artery thrombosis) which occasionally appears in the examination.

Notes

5. STATION 4 – COMMUNICATION SKILLS AND ETHICS

In this section of the examination you will be assessed on your ability to hold a consultation with a subject who may be a patient, a relative or a surrogate such as a health care worker, and to handle issues involving medical ethics. There is an interview for 14 minutes, followed, after the subject has left, by a five minute discussion of the case with the examiners.

You are being assessed on three basic areas in relation to the interview:

1. The conduct of the interview
2. Exploration and problem negotiation, leading to a clear course of action
3. Ethics and law

Listening skills

- Always introduce yourself – explain who you are and what you do. Usually it is polite to shake hands with the patient. Sit down, with the patient at eye level, be sure the patient is adequately dressed and comfortable. Relax!
- Use facilitation techniques to maximise listening: encourage the patient to talk – nod, maintain eye contact, tolerate short silences; repeat and reiterate key points in the discussion; reflect on what the patient is saying – with phrases such as 'if I understand you correctly...'

You will need to be able to demonstrate patience and diplomacy in dealing with uncooperative patients or relatives, and sensitivity to racial, cultural, generational, gender or religious differences.

Basics of an ethical decision

Ethical issues can often be well discussed in terms of the four basic principles :

1. Respect for patient autonomy
According to this principle, a health professional should help the patient make their own decisions by providing information, and respect and follow these decisions even when he does not agree with them.

2. Beneficience – promotion of what is best for the patient

The principle is often interpreted as focusing on what an objective assessment by a relevant health professional would determine as in the patient's best interests.

3. Non-malificience – avoiding harm

In practice, most treatments have potential for causing harm, and the risks and benefits must be weighed up to decide what is in the patient's best interests.

4. Justice – doing what is morally right

This principle implies that patients should normally have access to similar health care, and how resources should be distributed fairly between different groups of patients.

Under the principle of justice some also consider **legal aspects** to be included – **in any case mention and consideration of legal aspects needs to be taken into account in discussion of ethical issues in the PACES exam.**

Informed consent

Five essential prerequisites indicate **competence** or **capacity** to consent to treatment or non-treatment. These are encapsulated as:

(i) ability to understand a simple explanation of their condition, prognosis and proposed treatment or non-treatment;

(ii) reason consistently about specific goals linked to their personal beliefs;

(iii) choose to act on the basis of such reasoning;

(iv) communicate the substance of their choice and the reasons for that choice;

(v) understand the practical consequences of their choice.

NB. Each of these needs to be present for a sustained length of time for competence to be firmly established.

The underlying principles of consent in English law for patients aged 18 or over, i.e. adults, are:

For competent patients

- Patients may refuse any, even life-saving, treatment. If treatment is conducted without consent of patient, this constitutes battery.
- Patients must be given information about the nature and purpose of the intervention, risks including common and rare serious side effects, hoped-for benefits and reasonable alternatives.

Valid consent

As discussed by Hope[2] valid consent requires that:

- The doctor discloses information to a patient who is competent
- The patient understands the information and makes a decision voluntarily

Voluntary consent

As discussed by Alderson and Goodey[3] voluntary consent involves:

- Freedom from 'force, fraud, deceit, duress, overreaching, or other ulterior form of constraint or coercion
- Knowing about the right to refuse or withdraw, without prejudicing further health care
- The right to ask questions and to negotiate aspects of treatment which have been coerced perhaps by disease, but not by other people

For incompetent patients

- Doctors should act in the best interests of patients. In this case the doctor must use professional judgment to determine what is in the patient's best interests. The legal test is the so-called **'Bolam test'** after the case of the same name, in which it was concluded that *'a doctor is not negligent if he has acted in accordance with the practice accepted as proper by a responsible body of medical men skilled in that particular art'.*
- Relatives and friends of the patient may be sources of information when judging what is in the best interests of the patient, but **cannot give or withhold consent on behalf of a patient under English law.**

---

[2] Hope, T (2000), Consent in 'Ethics and Communication Skills', *Medicine* Vol 28:10, pp 5–9 The Medicine Publishing Company Ltd

[3] Alderson, P and Goodey, C (1998), Theories of Consent. *BMJ* 317: 1313–1315

As discussed in 'The Human face of Medicine'[4] not only is a doctor able to give treatment to an incapacitated patient when it is clearly in that patient's best interests, it is a common law duty to do so. Nevertheless, if a person is now incapacitated but is known to have objections to all or some treatment, doctors may not be justified in proceeding, even in an emergency. If the incapacity is temporary, because of anaesthetic, sedation, intoxication, or temporary unconsciousness, doctors should not proceed beyond what is essential to preserve the person's life or prevent deterioration in health.

Consent to research

Consent to research involves knowing about and understanding:

- The research purpose, questions, aims and methods
- Relevant terms such as 'randomise'
- The treatment, if any, which the research investigates
- Benefits, risks, harms or costs to research subjects
- Hoped-for benefits to other groups such as future patients
- Confidentiality, indemnity, sponsors, ethical approval
- The research team and a named contact

A further discussion of consent is found in 'Ethics in General Practice'.[5]

Confidentiality

As discussed by Lockwood[6] the General Medical Council guideline on confidentiality states that:
'patients have a right to expect that doctors will not disclose any personal information which they learn during the course of their professional duties, unless they give permission. Without assurances about confidentiality, patients may be reluctant to give doctors the information they need to provide good care'.

---

[4] Apollo, *The Human Face of Medicine* (2001) 2-CD distance learning program, *BMJ* Publishing Group, London

[5] Orme-Smith, A and Spicer, J (2001) *Ethics in General Practice*, Radcliffe Medical Press, Abingdon

[6] Lockwood, G (2000) 'Confidentiality' in 'Ethics and Communication Skills', *Medicine* Vol 28:10, pp 10–12 The Medicine Publishing Company Ltd

The GMC guidelines do not have the force of law, but are taken seriously by the courts. They state that disclosure may be necessary in the public interest when failure to disclose information may expose the patient, or others, to risk of death or serious harm. In such circumstances, you should disclose information promptly to an appropriate person or authority. Examples of such circumstances include a patient who continues to drive, against medical advice, when unfit to do so; when disclosure is necessary to prevent or detect a serious crime; or when a colleague, who is a patient, is placing patients at risk because of illness or another medical condition.

In the latter case, the 'non-functioning colleague' which may be discussed in the PACES, the priority must be given to patient care, with consideration for the colleague and Clinical Governance issues. You should not ignore the issue or try to deal with it on your own; you should consider discussing the situation in confidence with a senior colleague, and if appropriate the BMA.

Lockwood also lists examples of situations in which doctors may or may not breach confidentiality as follows:

Situations in which doctors **must not** breach confidentiality

- Casual breaches (e.g. for amusement, to satisfy curiosity)
- To prevent minor crime or help conviction in minor crime
- To prevent minor harm to another individual
- Doctors working in genitourinary clinics should not provide information to third parties that might identify a patient examined or treated for sexually transmitted diseases (except in a few specific situations)
- Doctors should not write a report or fill in a form disclosing confidential information (e.g. for an insurance company) without the patient's (preferably written) consent

Situations in which doctors **must** breach confidentiality (to specific authorities only)

- Notifiable diseases – Notifiable Diseases Act (1984)
- Drug addiction – Misuse of Drugs Act (1973)
- Termination of pregnancy – Abortion Act (1967)
- Births and deaths – Births and Deaths Registration Act (1953)

- To police on request – name and address (but not clinical details) of driver of vehicle who is alleged to be guilty of an offence under the Road Traffic Act (1988)
- Search warrant signed by circuit judge
- Under Court orders
- Identification of patients undergoing *in vitro* fertility treatment with donated gametes (and the outcome of such treatment) – Human Fertilisation and Embryology Act (1990)
- Identification of donors and recipients of transplanted organs – Human Organ Transplants Act (1989)
- Prevention, apprehension or prosecution of terrorists connected with Northern Ireland – Prevention of Terrorism Act (1989)

Situations in which doctors have *discretion* to breach confidentiality

- Sharing of information with other members of the health care team in the interests of the patient
- A patient who is not medically fit to drive continues to do so (note that the GMC now advises doctors to inform the DVLA medical officer in such circumstances)
- A third party is at significant risk of harm (e.g. partner of HIV-positive person)

ETHICS AND GENETIC SCREENING/COUNSELLING

Issues related to genetic screening are discussed by Campbell et al[7]. **Genetic screening is often regarded as having three goals:**

- It should contribute to improving the health of people with genetic disorders
- It allows carriers for an abnormal gene to make informed choices about reproduction
- It should help alleviate the anxieties of families and communities faced with the prospect of a genetic disease

---

[7] Campbell A, Charlesworth M, Gilett, G and Jones, G (1997), *Medical Ethics* Second Edn, Oxford University Press

Three key issues to be borne in mind are:

• **Need for prior consent**

Prior informed consent is needed before genetic screening because of emphasis on the autonomy of the individual. The patient has the right to refuse testing.

• **Confidentiality**

The results of screening must be confidential between the subject, the one who does the investigation and whoever commissions and interprets it. The patient can refuse third-person access to the information according to the principle of the right to privacy.

• **Need to avoid stigmatisation of genetically disadvantaged**

There should be no stigmatisation of patients with genetic disadvantages as long as confidentiality is maintained. There is the possibility that genetic testing could lead to workplace discrimination – again an issue only if compulsory genetic testing were applied.

Gene therapy/eugenics

You need to be able to discuss ethical aspects of **gene therapy**: is genetic technology tinkering with nature in a uniquely dangerous way? You must form and express your own views on this if asked in PACES. Some have argued that somatic cell gene therapy could represent the beginning of a slippery slope, its inevitable concomitant being germ line therapy and **eugenics**, a move to try to perfect the human species beyond curing diseases.

Euthanasia

As discussed by Savulescu[8] euthanasia originally meant 'a good death' (from the Greek 'eu thanatos'), free from pain and distress. More recently the term acquired the meaning of killing someone for their own benefit. Euthanasia in the latter sense remains illegal in the UK. Assisting suicide is also a criminal offence.

---

[8] Savulescu, J (2000) End-of-life decisions; in 'Ethics and Communication Skills' *Medicine* Vol 28:10, pp 13–16, The Medicine Publishing Company Ltd

Under English law, a competent patient can refuse any, ev treatment. Hence, the recent case of Miss B illustrates that **no uᴗᴗ can be given contrary to the wish of mentally competent patients even if it is necessary to save life. Indeed, competent adults can refuse treatments for reasons that are 'rational, irrational or for no reason'.** In this case, the patient (a 43-year-old woman paralysed after a spinal haemorrhage) complained that she was being treated by artificial ventilation, to keep her alive against her wishes. She won her case at the High Court on March 22nd 2002.

The **withdrawal of life prolonging treatment** is acceptable in some circumstances but should always be discussed with the consultant and Trust solicitor. The BMA has stated that:
'although emotionally it may be easier to withhold treatment than to withdraw that which has started, there are no legal or necessary morally relevant differences between the two actions'.

Treatment of incompetent patients must be in their best interests. There is no legal duty to preserve life at all costs. The law recognises that a patient's best interests may be best served by withholding treatment which would overall be burdensome, or by providing palliative treatment which could shorten life. However, it is illegal (and potentially murder) for a doctor to take action with the intention of shortening life.

The **doctrine of double effect** is a concept which you should be able to discuss: it attempts to distinguish between harms that are intended and harms that are foreseen but not intended. For example, a doctor may give a high dose of morphine to a patient with terminal cancer to relieve his pain, foreseeing that it may shorten his life by depressing respiration. According to the doctrine of double effect it would be morally wrong if the intention was to hasten death, but not necessarily wrong if the intention was to relieve pain with the foreseeable consequence of hastening death.

Do-not-resuscitate (DNR) orders

Because CPR must be performed urgently, a decision must be made **in advance** for all hospital patients whether resuscitation is appropriate should they suffer cardiac arrest. According to the BMA/RCN/UK guidelines a DNR decision may be considered in the circumstances listed on page 114.

- CPR is unlikely to be successful ('futile'). Possible definitions of futility include: likelihood of regaining consciousness after resuscitation <1%; likelihood of leaving hospital after resuscitation <10%; patient will only live for a few weeks because of an untreatable illness.
- CPR is not in accord with the recorded, sustained wishes of a patient who is mentally competent
- CPR is not in accordance with a valid **advance directive**. The latter is also known as a 'living will' and is a way for a patient to exert in effect autonomy at a time when he has become no longer competent to do so.
- Resuscitation is likely to be followed by a length and quality of life that would not be in the best interests of the patient

All patients have the right to be involved in DNR decisions, which are the responsibility of the consultant and should be linked to a Trust Policy. Where in doubt an attempt to resuscitate should be made.

Palliative care, quality of life

Palliation means to 'decrease the violence' of something, to 'moderate its intensity'. As stated by Purtilo[9] a rule of thumb is that stopping intense efforts to effect a cure must signal the beginning of an even more intense effort to engage in a regimen of clinical intervention aimed at reduction of pain and discomfort, maintaining quality of life as much as possible. This includes giving emotional support to people closest to the patient. These people may be very sad, or angry or confused and may transfer their feelings to you, at times questioning your own best judgment. Handling these situations requires great patience, sensitivity and compassion.

Artificial feeding in the unconscious patient

Nutritional support of the patient bereft of 'capacity' (in the legal sense of the word) is fertile ground for a discussion on ethics. In fact, it is relatively easy to apply the fundamental principles of medical ethics, namely autonomy, beneficence and non-maleficence (deliberate avoidance of harm), and justice, to two typical clinical scenarios as follows:

---

[9] Purtilo, R (1999), *Ethical Dimensions in the Health Professions*, W.B.Saunders Company, Philadelphia

The unconscious patient

The principle of justice mandates a judgment of outcome. A decision to feed is easy if there is good expectation of recovery with restored quality of life. Difficulties arise if recovery is uncertain, as is usually the case in clinical practice. A good compromise in these situations is the time limited trial of artificial feeding, where treatment targets and endpoints have to be formally assessed on a regular basis, e.g. once per week. A multidisciplinary approach to reviewing these targets, and the relatives should be actively included wherever possible.

By English law, it is the attending physician's responsibility to decide what the patient would have wanted had they been in a position to express a view. Clearly, no effort must be spared in making sure that patients' autonomy is respected. You must establish whether there is an advance patient directive (i.e. 'living will') in existence, written when the patient was in command of his faculties and fully *compos mentis*. In the absence of such a clear expression of the patient's will, the onus is on the doctor to act as the patient's advocate and surrogate decision maker, although it is important to take into consideration the views of close relatives who knew the patient well. Consideration of autonomy gives rise to interesting questions in these patients. In a patient who is unconscious or in a persistent vegetative state, we have to decide what they would have wanted if they were able to express an opinion.

Increasingly, a number of situations are emerging, where there is a strong consensus of medical opinion which regards non-treatment as legally and ethically justified.[10] Patients who lack capacity or can be said to be incompetent need not be treated actively when:

- death is imminent;
- extensive brain damage has permanently destroyed self-awareness and intentional action;
- there is loss of self-awareness, and so little motor ability, that sustained independent and intentional action is impossible;
- short and long-term memory is so damaged that the person who the patient originally was, has ceased to exist;
- there is severely limited understanding by the patient of distressing and marginally effective life-saving treatment that leads to a demonstrably awful life.

---

[10] Doyal L, Wilsher D, Withholding and withdrawing life sustaining treatment from elderly people: towards formal guidelines. *BMJ* 1994; 308:1689–1692

The terminally ill

Not all complex clinical dilemmas encountered will yield to the primary ethical principles outlined earlier. Whenever you have two doctors together, you usually have three opinions! Different doctors inevitably interpret many situations differently in terms of the emphasis they give to the various factors contributing to a particular clinical scenario. For example, evaluating concepts such as quality of life is largely subjective. The patient who is terminally ill could live days, weeks or months. When death is clearly days away, it would be entirely reasonable to consider tube feeding or parenteral feeding futile, and therefore an unjustifiable intrusion. Nevertheless, even here, any judgment will have to take into account the wishes of the patient.

There can no longer be much doubt that preventing the deleterious effects of malnutrition, even in terminal malignancy, will improve quality of life. The consequences of cancer cachexia are evident to most people, and most doctors would agree that if terminally ill patients can be spared the worst ravages of this in their last few months of life, it must be justified. Clearly, if it is ethically appropriate to use drugs to alleviate suffering in these patients, including appetite stimulants such as anabolic steroids, then according to the same logic, it must be possible to justify some form of nutritional support in these patients.

We would contend, that while it is a matter of individual clinical judgment how these issues are resolved in any particular case, and how long it is appropriate for a patient to live with their disease without receiving appropriate care, that there should be a full and frank discussion with the patients and their relatives. Some patients will be prepared to consider active nutritional support, particularly enteral nutrition by tube feeding rather than intravenous nutrition. However, many others will not.

Breaking bad news

This is a difficult aspect of a physician's work, and how to handle it is a very individual matter. However, certain key principles apply. Bad news is bad news, and cannot be made into good news. The key is to manage the speed of transition of the patient's perception from that of thinking he is well to the realisation that he has a life-threatening disease. If this transition occurs too abruptly, the patient will not be able to handle it psychologically, will have difficulties to adapt and will often go into a state of denial.

Buckman has described three stages of dying in a patient's mind:

- An initial stage in which the patient faces the threat, and experiences many emotions including fear, anxiety, shock, disbelief, anger, denial, guilt, humour, hope/despair, bargaining
- A chronic stage of being ill, in which the patient experiences resolution, diminished intensity of emotions or depression
- A final stage of acceptance

The following is a multi-step approach to breaking bad news, which may prove useful:

1. **Preparation:** know all the facts, arrange for doctor and nurse to both be present, set time aside for the discussion.
2. **Find out what the patient knows:** encourage the patient to give you a narrative – for example you may ask 'how did it all start?', followed by 'what happened next?' From this narrative you should start to appreciate the patient's level of understanding, main concerns, beliefs and expectations for the future.
3. **Find out if the patient wants more information:** this involves 'testing the waters' by asking a question such as 'would you like me to tell you something about your illness?' If the answer is clearly yes, you may move to step five, where bad news is broken.
4. **Allow denial:** denial is a powerful coping strategy. Use empathic questions to check for denial such as 'how do you feel things have been going?', or 'what have you been thinking about your illness?', or 'have you considered it might be serious?'
5. **Give a 'warning shot':** (e.g. 'I am afraid your illness is serious'). According to the patient's reaction, be more explicit.
6. **Break the news:** you must use clear simple language, avoiding medical jargon, checking the patient's understanding. Use kind words and be as optimistic as possible. Know when to stop – the patient may not remember too many details at this point.
7. **Pause: wait for the patient's response:** if there is excessive information or premature reassurance at this point, patients will often feel dissatisfied. The patient must be given the chance to express his concerns.
8. **Assess and focus on the patient's feelings and concerns:** ask the patient to name his feelings – 'how does this leave you feeling at this point?'. Empathy is more therapeutic than sympathy. You must allow the patient time for thought.

9. **Make a summary and plan:** taking into account the patient's
    concerns, support available and knowledge of the treatment options
    available. The plan should avoid unrealistic promises, but be
    optimistic – hoping for the best.
10. **Assure follow up:** be available for further questions and to support
    the patient during emotional adjustment. Plan to meet the patient's
    relatives. Realise that adjustment to bad news takes time. Patients
    may pass through different stages of acceptance from initial shock
    and numbness, to denial, then anger, then grief and perhaps finally
    acceptance.

Acquiring consent for autopsy

Acquiring consent for autopsy from the patient's next of kin is a difficult
task which must be handled most sensitively – you may be tested on this
in the communication skills and ethics station. Depending on the case you
may have to explain that it would be helpful to have an autopsy to be more
certain as to exactly what happened to cause the loved one's death.
Remember that if the cause of death is violence, injury, neglect, surgery,
anaesthesia, alcohol, suicide, poisoning, **or is unknown**, you must inform
the coroner, who may insist on performance of an autopsy.

Examples of cases

*   You are asked to break news of multiple sclerosis to a patient.

*   You are asked to break bad news of metastatic breast cancer to a
    patient and discuss further treatment. Patient is unhappy about
    previous treatment, wishes to discuss euthanasia.

*   You see the father of an 18-year-old boy who has suddenly died
    while playing football, and need to ask him for permission to
    perform a post mortem examination. Father extremely upset and
    quite angry. Issues include discussing legal aspects, including need
    to inform coroner. Exploration of issues re religion (patient Jewish)
    and requirements for burial.

*   You see a 32-year-old woman with two small children, with a history of
    multi-drug resistant TB. She was admitted to isolation for three months
    then stopped therapy. She has been re-admitted, further sputum samples
    are positive for AFB. You are the A&E SHO and must discuss with the
    patient the following: the tests required for investigation of any

underlying disease, the need to be admitted, the need for treatment, what the situation means to/for her children. Discussion might centre on whether you would normally discuss HIV early on, length of treatment, what to do if patient refused to be admitted? What to do if she refuses to be tested for HIV and refuses to have her children tested for TB?

- Discussion with the daughter of an 80-year-old man who has a metastatic Ca. lung carcinoma who has been admitted with SOB, anorexia and has swollen left leg. A DVT and pulmonary embolus suspected, but patient has declined treatment. Discussion of the prognosis, investigation, treatment and resuscitation status. You will be asked about patient's autonomy and how would you talk to him.

6. STATION 5 – SKIN, LOCOMOTOR SYSTEM, ENDOCRINE SYSTEM AND EYES

6.1 SKIN

Dermatological short cases

Many dermatological short cases are 'spot' diagnoses but others may be more difficult and if unsure you should give differential diagnoses. In all cases you must give a clear, accurate description of the lesion using recognised dermatological terms, the meaning of which you must understand.

Few candidates will have worked in this specialty so it is wise to arrange to sit in on some dermatology clinics before the clinical. If possible, on these occasions, practise describing each patient's lesions to the consultant and making your own diagnosis before he tells you what it is. You will rapidly become familiar with the terminology and the appearance of the common lesions.

The following is a list of terms which you should be able to use accurately.

Dermatological terms

Bulla	A blister > 5 mm in diameter
Crust	An accumulation of dried exudate
Ecchymosis	A large extravasation of blood
Erythema	Redness due to increased skin perfusion
Excoriation	A shallow abrasion due to scratching
Lichenification	Areas of increased epidermal thickness and accentuated skin markings secondary to chronic rubbing
Macule	A flat, circumscribed area of discoloration
Nodule	A palpable mass > 1 cm in diameter
Papule	A circumscribed elevation of the skin < 1 cm in diameter

Petechiae	Small purpuric lesions (< 2 mm in diameter)
Plaque	A flat topped palpable disc shaped lesion
Purpura	Discoloration of the skin or mucosa due to extravasation of red cells NB. Does not blanch on pressure.
Pustule	A visible accumulation of free pus
Scale	A flake of easily-detached keratin
Sclerosis	Induration of the dermis or subcutaneous tissues
Telangiectasia	Permanently dilated, visible small vessels
Ulcer	An excavation due to loss of tissue, including the epidermal surface
Vesicle	A circumscribed fluid-containing elevation less than 5 mm in diameter
Weal	An area of dermal oedema; usually transient, raised, white, compressible, with a pink margin

Notes

ECZEMA

Remember the cardinal signs: erythema, papules, vesicles, hyperkeratosis with scaling, exudation of serum (weeping) and crusting. Excoriations and lichenification may be present.

Revise and make notes on the different types of eczema listed below:

Exogenous: Primary irritant
                  Allergic

Endogenous: Atopic
                  Seborrhoeic
                  Gravitational (varicose)
                  Asteatotic
                  Discoid (nummular)
                  Pompholyx on hand and foot

Be ready to discuss the treatment of eczema in both the acute and chronic forms.

Notes

PSORIASIS

This is a common short case. Remember the classical description: raised, red, circular or oval plaques with sharply marginated edges and a scaly surface.

Look for involvement in the commonest sites first, to show that you are familiar with these:

- Extensor aspects of knees and elbows
- Sacral area
- Scalp (especially behind ears)

Proceed to look for nail changes:

- Thimble-pitting
- Onycholysis (occasionally with green discoloration due to chromogenic bacteria)
  - Other causes include trauma, fungal infection, thyrotoxicosis and drugs e.g. cloxacillin
- Thickening and ridging of the nail-plate

Look for evidence of arthropathy in both the small (especially distal interphalangeal) and large joints (see psoriatic arthropathy p. 146)

Remember the variants which may occur:

- Guttate
- Pustular
- Flexural
- Erythrodermic

As with eczema it is not uncommon to be asked to give a brief account of the treatment of psoriasis and you should revise this carefully.

Notes

LICHEN PLANUS

This is occasionally used as a spot diagnosis case. You must be able to recognise the classical purplish, flat-topped, shiny, polygonal papules.

- Look for Wickham's striae over the lesions

- Show that you are aware of the common distribution by looking especially at the flexor aspects of the wrists, trunk and lower limbs

- Look for lesions in the mouth (found in 25% of cases)

- Look for nail changes: pits, ridges, splits or even complete nail loss

- Ask if you may take a drug history (e.g. chloroquine and gold may cause a lichen planus-like reaction)

Remember that, like psoriasis and warts, lichen planus exhibits Koebner's phenomenon (occurring in sites of scratching or other injury)

Notes

ROSACEA

You will be asked to 'Look at the patient's face'. You must be able to recognise the characteristic lesions: papules, pustules, erythema and telangiectasia over the cheeks, nose, forehead and chin.

You must look carefully for eye complications: usually keratitis but occasionally blepharitis, conjunctivitis, iritis and even episcleritis.

Revise the treatment of the condition.

Some candidates confuse this with the butterfly rash of SLE. Remember that in the latter condition there are no papules or pustules, but unlike rosacea, there may be scaling and follicular plugging.

Notes

PITYRIASIS ROSEA

Remember that the lesions are usually oval and occur on the trunk, macules tending to be aligned along the skin creases. Look for a 'herald patch' on the trunk and check lesions for centripetal scaling.

Notes

LUPUS ERYTHEMATOSUS

A. Systemic

Butterfly rash is a common spot diagnosis ('Look at the face').

- Look for a symmetrical rash with erythema, scaling, telangiectasia and follicular plugging. Chronic lesions may show hyperpigmentation and atrophy.

- Inspect other areas exposed to sunlight, especially arms, for rash

- Look for evidence of oral ulceration (present in 30% of cases)

Before proceeding further, it may be as well to state the diagnosis and the signs. You should then ask the examiner if you may examine:

a) The scalp for alopecia
b) The hands for: erythema of thenar or hypothenar areas
   dilated nail-fold capillaries, periungual
   infarcts and splinter haemorrhages
c) The elbows and knees for erythema, telangiectasia and scaling

You may ask if you may take a drug history (e.g. hydralazine).

Remember that other rashes may occur in SLE, e.g. livedo reticularis, urticaria, purpura due to thrombocytopenia, vasculitic rashes, pyoderma gangrenosum.

You are unlikely to be asked to proceed to general examination in the short cases but you should have a scheme for doing so just in case.

Notes

B. Discoid

The scaly red plaques with follicular plugging may be shown as a short case. As well as on the face (the most common site) look for lesions on the scalp (there may be scarring alopecia), ears, neck and hands.

Look for crusting and erosions of the lips.

Remember that scarring is more a feature of discoid than of systemic lupus and you should comment on this if it is present.

You may be asked about the relationship of discoid LE to the systemic form: remember that only 5% of cases of discoid LE convert to the systemic form, whereas up to 33% of cases of SLE have discoid-type lesions at some time during the course of the disease.

Notes

XANTHOMATA

These are commonly shown as a spot diagnosis case, which you should recognise immediately and go on to look for associations. The following is a simplified guide. You must be fully conversant with the classification, investigation and treatment of hyperlipidaemia

Tendon xanthomata
The candidate may be asked to 'Look at these hands.' Tendon xanthomata classically occur in the extensor tendons and may become more obvious when the patient clenches his fist.

Look also for xanthomata in the Achilles tendons and patellar tendons.

Look for xanthelasmata and corneal arcus.

Remember that tendon xanthomata are classically found in Type IIA lipoproteinaemia: this may be primary (familial hypercholesterolaemia), or secondary (seen in jaundice).

Xanthelasmata
This time the candidate may be invited to 'Examine the eyes'. Never forget the importance of inspection. Look for corneal arcus, which often coexists with xanthelasmata and is typically most pronounced at the 12 and 6 o'clock positions (in contrast to corneal calcification which tends to be maximal at the 3 and 9 o'clock positions).

Look for tendon xanthomas in the hands and Achilles tendons (see above). Check the palms for xanthomata (see palmar xanthomata overleaf) and tell the examiners that you would like to take the patient's blood pressure and test the urine for glucose (hypertension and diabetes mellitus being associated with Type IIB lipoproteinaemia).

Remember that xanthelasmata and corneal arcus may occur in:

* Normal people
* Type IIA lipoproteinaemia (see tendon xanthomata above)
* Type IIB lipoproteinaemia (mixed hyperlipidaemia)
* Type III lipoproteinaemia

Eruptive xanthomata
You should be able to recognise the multiple red or yellow vesicles which are found on extensor surfaces: back, buttocks, elbows, knees. These are not usually associated with tendon xanthomata or xanthelasmata.

Ask if you may inspect the fundi for lipaemia retinalis (found in severe hyperlipidaemia) and test the urine for glucose.

Eruptive xanthomata classically occur in lipoproteinaemia Type IV (familial hypertriglyceridaemia, which may be associated with diabetes mellitus and obesity. It also occurs in Types I and V lipoproteinaemia.

Palmar xanthomata
These rare xanthomata could also be shown as a spot diagnosis case, the orange or yellow discolorations of the palmar and digital creases being most distinctive. Look also for 'tubo-eruptive xanthomata' characteristically found over the knees and elbows.

Check the eyelids for xanthelasmata, which are also associated.

Palmar and tubo-eruptive xanthomata strongly suggest the presence of remnant hyperlipoproteinaemia (Type III).

Notes

BULLOUS DISORDERS

Revise the features and associations of the following rashes which occasionally occur as short cases:

Dermatitis herpetiformis: look for characteristic distribution on extensor surface of elbows, knees and on occiput, interscapular and gluteal regions.

Pemphigus: lesions in mouth common. Bullae tend to break easily. Widespread crusting and erosions.

Pemphigoid: mucosal ulceration rare. Tense bullae present with erythematous plaques.

Erythema multiforme: pleomorphic eruption (macules, papules, bullae). Look for target lesions and for lesions in the mouth. NB. Stevens-Johnson syndrome, a severe form with fever, arthralgia, orogenital and conjunctival involvement.

Notes

NEUROFIBROMATOSIS

Be able to demonstrate the various skin lesions (fibromata, plexiform neurofibromata, café-au-lait spots, axillary freckles) and have a scheme for general examination, e.g. check hearing (acoustic neuroma), visual acuity and fundi (optic glioma), look for kyphoscoliosis, ask to check blood pressure (phaeochromocytoma).

Revise the other complications.

Notes

ADENOMA SEBACEUM

Know the other skin manifestations of tuberose sclerosis: 'ash leaf' depigmented macules on trunk; 'shagreen patch' on lower trunk; periungual fibromata. Ask if you may inspect fundi for phakomata.

Other associations: lung and kidney hamartomas, cardiac rhabdomyoma, polycystic kidneys, cerebral glioma (patient may have craniotomy scar). Epilepsy and mental retardation are other features.

Notes

LUPUS PERNIO

A rare short case. Other skin manifestations of sarcoidosis: erythema nodosum (in acute form of disease), scar infiltration, granuloma of nose, brownish nodules (micropapular sarcoid), sarcoid plaques of limbs, shoulders, buttocks and thighs.

Notes

LESIONS ON THE LEGS

Necrobiosis lipoidica diabeticorum

A common 'spot' case. Associated with diabetes in about 75% of cases; the related granuloma annulare is much less predictably associated. Revise the histology of these lesions (occasionally asked): collagen degeneration with surrounding epithelioid and giant cells.

Pretibial myxoedema

Remember to check for thyroid acropachy, exophthalmos/ocular palsies, goitre/thyroidectomy scar.

Erythema nodosum

Revise the causes: streptococcal sore throat, sarcoidosis, drugs, viral and chlamydial infection, and tuberculosis are the commonest causes in Britain. Remember though that Crohn's disease and ulcerative colitis are common associations in teaching hospital practice. You are likely to be asked how you would investigate the case.

Notes

LEG ULCERS

The three commonest forms are:

- **Venous ulceration:** usually over medial malleolus; gently sloping edge; may be eczema surrounding the area with pigmentation, sclerosis (atrophie blanche).

- **Ischaemic:** painful punched out ulcer: commonly on toes dorsum of feet, shins and around malleoli.

- **Neuropathic:** painless punched out ulcer often on soles of feet or heels (e.g. diabetes, spina bifida). Charcot's arthropathy may be present. NB. In diabetes, ischaemia and neuropathy often both contribute to ulceration often with superadded infection.

Examination:
After describing the ulcer, look for signs of poor peripheral perfusion and test the peripheral pulses. If you suspect neuropathic ulcer (commonly shown) test for sensory neuropathy and say that you would like to test the patient's urine for sugar.

Remember that an everted edge occurs in squamous cell carcinoma e.g. Marjolin's ulcer.

In a negroid patient do not forget the possibility of sickle cell anaemia. Ulcers also occur with hereditary spherocytosis.

Other rarer causes to bear in mind include vasculitis in systemic lupus erythematosus (look for butterfly rash) and rheumatoid arthritis (especially with Felty's syndrome).

A special case, also occurring on the trunk, buttocks, upper limbs and face, is pyoderma gangrenosum, an irregular ulcer with an overhanging purple edge and necrotic base.

Causes of pyoderma gangrenosum:
- Inflammatory bowel disease (especially ulcerative colitis)
- Benign monoclonal gammopathy
- Rheumatoid arthritis
- Leukaemia

Rare causes of ulcers include gumma, tuberculosis and hypertension (Martorell's ulcer).

Notes

LEG OEDEMA

A common case. Look to see whether the oedema is unilateral or bilateral. Test for pitting. Look for sacral oedema. Non-pitting oedema may occur with 'lipoedema' due to long-standing oedema of any cause, but remember Milroy's disease (primary lymphoedema), which is often asymmetrical. (Filariasis may cause a similar picture.)

In bilateral oedema look for:

- Signs of right heart failure, especially raised jugular venous pressure

- Involvement of the face/periorbital tissues suggests nephrotic syndrome (ask to test patient's urine for protein)

- Signs of chronic liver disease (hypoalbuminaemia may occur, look especially for leuconychia)

- Palpate inguinal nodes for enlargement; malignant infiltration may cause secondary lymphoedema

- Comment on the desirability of abdominal, rectal and vaginal examination to exclude malignancy. Remember that bilateral iliac vein thrombosis may cause bilateral oedema, as may pregnancy.

In unilateral oedema look for:

- Other signs of deep venous thrombosis

- Measure the calf with a tape-measure

- Look for varicose veins, venous eczema and ulceration

An important differential diagnosis of calf swelling is a ruptured Baker's cyst, consider this especially in a patient with osteoarthritis or rheumatoid arthritis (a common discussion point). Ultrasound, arthrography and/or venography may be required to distinguish between the two conditions, which may even coexist. Milroy's disease must again be considered in the differential.

Finally note that cellulitis may produce inflammatory oedema as well as lymphatic oedema due to lymphangitis; look for the latter as well as lymphadenopathy in the inguinal region.

Notes

KAPOSI'S SARCOMA

There may be solitary or numerous reddy-purple, and bluish-brown macules, plaques and nodules. They may occur on the skin and mucosa. The condition is endemic in elderly African males, with mainly peripheral rather than mucosal involvement and good response to chemotherapy. In HIV +ve patients the distribution may be widespread. There may be lymphatic obstruction leading to chronic oedema and cellulitis of the lower limbs. Pulmonary Kaposi's sarcoma may present as breathlessness.

The condition is also seen in elderly Jewish or Mediterranean males, with an indolent course on the distal extremities, and in immunodeficient patients including transplant patients. Treatment is specialised and may involve radiotherapy, interferon alpha and chemotherapy.

Notes

HEREDITARY HAEMORRHAGIC TELANGIECTASIA

More often shown as a slide in the written section but occasionally used as a short case, 'Look at this patient's face'. Look for telangiectases not only on the face and lips but also on the conjunctivae and in the mouth. Look also for involvement of the fingers. You may be allowed to ask questions (family history, GI bleeding, etc.). Revise the complications.

Notes

PURPURA

Occasionally shown as a short case: revise the causes; remember that these fall largely into two groups:

- Vessel disorders
- Platelet disorders

Note that coagulation disorders tend to produce large ecchymoses rather than purpura.

You should:

a) Observe the distribution of the lesions e.g.

- Senile purpura/steroids often affect backs of hands and forearms

- Henoch-Schönlein purpura classically appears over lower limbs and buttocks

- Scurvy over lower limbs/backs of thighs with perifollicular haemorrhages plus corkscrew hairs; look for swollen gums (other causes of gum hypertrophy: phenytoin, monocytic leukaemia).

b) Inspect: Palate for petechial haemorrhages
Gums for ulceration and haemorrhage (suggests neutropenia and thrombocytopenia of e.g. leukaemia).

c) Inspect conjunctivae and fundi for haemorrhages (fundal haemorrhages only in severe thrombocytopenia).

d) Look for evidence of cause:

- ? Cushingoid (ask for history of steroid ingestion)
- ? Rheumatoid arthritis, systemic lupus erythematosus, infective endocarditis. Note that vasculitic lesions tend to be discrete, raised and polychromatic
- ? Chronic liver disease (thrombocytopenia may occur though coagulopathy due to hypoprothrombinaemia is more common)
- ? Elastic skin/hyperextensible joints (Ehlers-Danlos syndrome)

Ask if you may examine for enlargement of liver, spleen or nodes (NB. spleen is often impalpable or only just palpable in idiopathic thrombocytopenic purpura, a common cause).

Remember to include disseminated intravascular coagulation (e.g. due to meningococcal septicaemia) in your differential diagnosis.

Notes

VITILIGO

Occasionally shown as a discussion case: revise the associations and modes of treatment.

Notes

ACANTHOSIS NIGRICANS

Another spot diagnosis: look for characteristic distribution: axillae, groins, umbilicus, nipples. You will be asked the associations:

- Obesity
- Internal malignancy (usually adenocarcinoma)
- Endocrine causes:
  - Diabetes mellitus
  - Cushing's syndrome
  - Acromegaly
  - Polycystic ovary syndrome
  - Congenital partial lipodystrophy (see p. 161)

Notes

HERPES ZOSTER

Macules progressing to papules and vesicles develop in a dermatomal distribution, leading to crusting and scars especially in elderly or middle-aged patients. The commonest distribution is in a thoracic dermatome, with cranial nerve involvement – especially the ophthalmic division of the trigeminal nerve, next commonest. Complications include postherpetic neuralgia (10%) and peripheral motor and cranial nerve palsies – especially facial nerve palsy (including **Ramsay Hunt** syndrome – herpes zoster of the external auditory meatus and geniculate ganglion: taste to the anterior two-thirds of the tongue is lost; there may be lesions on the fauces and palate).

Notes

NAIL CHANGES

You must be able to recognise nail changes including onycholysis, pitting and **Beau's lines**, transverse furrows which can occur after any systemic illness.

Notes

6.2 LOCOMOTOR SYSTEM

Revise your method of examining large joints, especially the hip, knee and ankle joints, as you will occasionally be asked to do this in the clinical. Be sure that you can examine the spine and sacroiliac joints proficiently.

EXAMINATION OF ARTHRITIC HANDS

Ask the patient's permission to examine his hands and then observe carefully for joint swelling and deformities. The pattern of joint involvement is all important and should be carefully noted.

Look for characteristic rheumatoid deformities:

* Swan-neck
* Boutonnière
* Z-deformity of thumb
* Ulnar deviation of fingers
* Dorsal subluxation of ulna at carpal joint

Ask the patient whether his hands are painful before touching them. Then pick up the hands and examine:

* Nails for thimble-pitting or nail fold infarcts
* Clubbing as in hypertrophic pulmonary osteoarthropathy (NB. wrists)
* Temperature over joints

Check for:

* Rheumatoid nodules
* Heberden's or Bouchard's nodules
* Gouty tophi
* Synovial effusions in tendon sheaths

Observe and palpate for wasting of the small muscles of the hand. Note whether the skin is atrophic (often secondary to steroid therapy).

Turn the hand over so that the palm faces upwards and observe for palmar erythema (see p. 28).

Look quickly at the elbows for psoriatic plaques or rheumatoid nodules and if you suspect gout, look at the helices of the ears for tophi.

Test the grip and pincer movements, and quickly test for evidence of median or ulnar nerve compression. (Test abductor pollicis brevis and interossei and compare sensation with pinprick over index and little fingers.)

Get the patient to perform a simple test of hand function, such as undoing a button or writing.

RHEUMATOID ARTHRITIS

Usually you will be asked to 'Examine these hands' (see previous page).

Although this is unlikely as a short case be prepared to look for evidence of systemic complications (especially ocular, cardiac, pulmonary and neurological) and devise a scheme for doing this rapidly.

Felty's syndrome occasionally occurs as a short case, the candidate being asked to palpate the abdomen (where he should find splenomegaly).

Notes

ANKYLOSING SPONDYLITIS

Be sure to revise your methods of examining the spine and sacroiliac joints during your preparation for the clinical.

Advanced cases may have the classic 'question mark' spine, with thoracic kyphosis, hyperextension of the neck and loss of lumbar lordosis. Chest expansion may be limited due to fusion of the costovertebral joints.

Examine the spine: in early cases (patient is typically a young male) there is restriction of movement in the lumbar spine especially lateral flexion but also forward flexion. This may be gauged by measuring the increase in distance between two fingers placed on the top and bottom of the lumbar spine while holding a tape measure: the distance should 'expand' by over 5 cm on forward flexion. There may also be diminution of rotation (thoracic spine involvement) and flattening of the lumbar lordosis.

Test for sacroiliac pain: use several methods but always include 'springing the pelvis' and pushing the flexed knee towards the opposite shoulder (watch the patient's face and be careful not to cause excessive pain while doing this).

Measure chest expansion: less than 2 cm is pathological.

Look for:

- Peripheral arthropathy, especially large joints e.g. knees, ankles (10%)
- Tenderness over Achilles tendons (tendonitis)
- Iritis (20%)

Ask the examiner if you may:

- Examine heart for aortic regurgitation (1%)
- Examine lungs for apical fibrosis (1%)

Notes

REITER'S DISEASE

The patient is usually a young male. Remember that although the arthritis is usually polyarticular the diagnosis must be considered when a patient presents just with a large swollen knee joint (see p. 149).

After examining affected joints, test for sacroiliac tenderness (sacroiliitis in 20% of cases) and for tenderness over the Achilles tendon and plantar fascia. Look for keratoderma blennorrhagica on the soles and palms and for evidence of conjunctivitis or iritis (the latter occurs with repeated attacks).

Look in the mouth for ulcers and tell the examiner that you would like to inspect the genitalia for circinate balanitis.

Tell the examiner that you would like to know whether the patient has any history of urethral discharge (chlamydial infection) or diarrhoea (Salmonella, Shigella, Yersinia, Campylobacter).

Notes

PSORIATIC ARTHROPATHY

A popular case. The distal arthropathy of the hands is often presented. Thimble-pitting of the nails and plaques of psoriasis at the elbow or elsewhere should not escape your attention.

Remember the five different forms of psoriatic arthropathy:

1. Asymmetrical distal interphalangeal joint involvement (usually with nail changes)
2. Seronegative rheumatoid-like pattern
3. Oligoarthritis
4. Arthritis mutilans
5. Ankylosing spondylitis-like pattern

Notes

SCLERODERMA

A common short case ('Look at these hands'). Look for the characteristic skin features in the hands:

- Thickening and tightening of the skin which may appear shiny (dermal atrophy). Early cases show only oedema.

- Subcutaneous calcification (usually localised to finger tips but may involve extensor aspects of forearms or elbows)

- Ulceration over bony eminences and calcific deposits (look especially at finger-tips)

- There may be areas of increased pigmentation and/or vitiligo

- Look for polyarthropathy (25%, though arthralgia is much more common) in small joints which may mimic rheumatoid arthritis

- Look at the face for microstomia with radiating fissures and telangiectases on cheeks and lip margins

- Look for alopecia which may occur. If allowed to ask questions enquire about Raynaud's phenomenon and dysphagia. Revise the systemic complications.

Occasionally morphoea may be shown; revise the appearance.

Notes

GOUT

Acute gout is unlikely to be shown unless there is a classical case on the ward. Chronic tophaceous gout may appear, however, the usual case being the asymmetrical arthropathy of the hands.

Remember to look for tophi in the periarticular tissues, bursae (especially olecranon bursa), tendon sheaths and helices of the ears.

Notes

PAINFUL SWOLLEN KNEE JOINT

Practise your methods of demonstrating fluid within the joint. Watch the patient while doing this and be careful not to hurt him/her.

Be ready with a list of causes. You may find it useful to expand the following list:

Trauma infections:	Septic arthritis
	Gonococcal or meningococcal infection
	Rheumatic fever
	Viral infections

Seronegative arthropathies:	Reiter's disease
	Reactive arthropathy
	Ankylosing spondylitis
	Psoriatic arthropathy
	Enteropathic arthropathy

| Metabolic: | Gout |
| | Pseudogout (associated with hyperparathyroidism, hyperuricaemia and gout, haemochromatosis, acromegaly, diabetes mellitus, renal failure, Wilson's disease, ochronosis) |

| Haematological: | Haemophilia |
| | Sickle cell anaemia |

Osteoarthritis

Rheumatoid disease

When discussing your management always mention the importance of aspiration of the joint and culture of the fluid for bacterial infection/microscopy for crystals.

Notes

6.3 ENDOCRINE/METABOLIC CASES

'EXAMINE THE PATIENT'S NECK (OR THYROID GLAND)'

Ask permission to examine the patient and ensure that the neck is adequately exposed.

Observe:

- Is the jugular venous pressure elevated? (see p. 44)
- Are there any scars?
- Are there any enlarged lymph glands visible? If so, proceed to examine the neck glands thoroughly (see lymphadenopathy p. 151)
- Is there an obvious goitre? (the commonest example of this short case)

If there is an obvious goitre:

- Arrange the patient comfortably in a chair
- Give the patient a glass of water, there is usually one conveniently nearby! Inspect and palpate the gland from the front.
- Stand behind the patient and palpate the gland, one lobe at a time. The patient should be asked to swallow some water, at appropriate intervals.

You should be assessing:

- Size
- Texture: smooth or nodular; solitary or multiple nodules
- Mobility
- Tenderness

Palpate the cervical lymph glands.

- Check for tracheal displacement
- Percuss for retrosternal extension
- If there is a thyroidectomy scar, test for Chvostek's sign
- Auscultate over the gland for bruits

Now perform simple tests of thyroid function:

- Observe for myxoedematous facies
- Feel pulse (check rate, rhythm and volume)
- Feel palms (? sweaty). Look for palmar erythema.
- Ask patient to hold hands outstretched. Look for postural tremor.
- Inspect for acropachy
- Test supinator jerks (observe relaxation phase)
- Test for thyroid eye disease. Look for exophthalmos; test for ophthalmoplegia (use white hat pin) and lid lag.
- If you suspect hyperthyroidism, test for proximal myopathy by testing shoulder abduction
- Observe shins: ? pretibial myxoedema
- Tell the examiner that you would like to ask the patient if he has any difficulty in breathing or swallowing

LYMPHADENOPATHY

Enlarged cervical lymph glands are common as a short case. Look for a scar from lymph node biopsy and for radiotherapy markings.

Now examine methodically the deep cervical, tonsillar, submandibular, submental, occipital, posterior triangle and supraclavicular nodes.

Always look in the mouth for:

- Pharyngitis and palatal petechiae (seen in infectious mononucleosis)
- Tonsillar infiltration (sometimes seen in chronic lymphocytic leukaemia)
- Primary malignancies

If allowed, proceed to examine for generalised lymphadenopathy (palpate axillary, epitrochlear and inguinal nodes) and for enlargement of the liver and spleen. Comment on the desirability of clinical and radiological examination of the chest (TB or carcinoma).

When asked the differential diagnosis, consider common causes first:

- Localised cervical lymphadenopathy
- Infection: tonsillitis, tuberculosis
- Lymphoma, especially Hodgkin's
- Secondary carcinoma. Remember nasopharyngeal carcinoma which

may need to be excluded by ENT examination.

NB. Troisier's sign (Virchow's nodes): enlargement of left supraclavicular nodes suggestive of carcinoma of the stomach.

Generalised lymphadenopathy

Common causes are:

* Lymphomas
* Chronic lymphocytic leukaemia
* Infections
  Acute: infection mononucleosis; cytomegalovirus; toxoplasmosis
  Chronic: tuberculosis; brucellosis; syphilis (now rare)

Other causes worth remembering are phenytoin and AIDS.

Always include in your differential diagnosis both systemic lupus erythematosus (look for butterfly rash), and sarcoidosis (look for skin lesions, e.g. erythema nodosum).

Notes

CUSHING'S SYNDROME

The candidate is usually asked to 'Look at the patient's face'. The typical moon-face is usually striking. There may be plethora (polycythaemia), hirsutism and acne.

Look for:

- Truncal obesity, interscapular fat accumulation (buffalo hump) and thin legs. Be able to distinguish this from obesity due to dietary indiscretion.

- Purple striae on the abdomen, around the shoulders and breasts and on the thighs. (Striae gravidarum are typically silvery.)

- Evidence of easy bruising, and kyphosis (collapse of osteoporotic vertebrae).

Test muscle power at shoulders and hips for evidence of proximal myopathy. Tell the examiners that you would like to measure the patient's blood pressure and test the urine for sugar, and that you would like to know whether he (or she) is taking steroids.

Notes

THYROID DISEASE

See the suggested scheme for examination of the thyroid (p. 150). Modify this to suit your own taste and practise it until you can perform it smoothly and rapidly.

Practise palpating different goitres. The firm, rubbery goitre of Hashimoto's thyroiditis is a common case. Occasionally 'classical' patients with the triad of thyroid acropachy, pretibial myxoedema and thyroid eye disease appear in the examination. Always look for these.

Patients with solitary nodules may also appear. You may be asked how you would investigate any of these cases.

Notes

ADDISON'S DISEASE

The candidate is asked to look at a patient with generalised hyperpigmentation.

Look quickly for classical predominance of hyperpigmentation in:

- Exposed areas
- Friction areas (under straps or rings)
- Hand creases

Now inspect the lips, gums and buccal mucosa for pigmented areas.

If the patient is undressed look for adrenalectomy scars (Nelson's syndrome).

Remember that vitiligo may occur in association with Addison's disease, producing a very characteristic picture of areas of both increased and decreased pigmentation.

You may be invited to ask the patient some questions: ask about any history of fatigue, anorexia, weight loss, nausea, abdominal pain or diarrhoea.

Revise the list of causes of diffuse hyperpigmentation
- Endocrine: Addison's disease, Nelson's syndrome, thyrotoxicosis, acromegaly.
- Metabolic: liver disease (e.g. prolonged cholestasis), haemochromatosis, chronic renal failure, porphyria cutanea tarda, pellagra
- Drugs: chlorpromazine (slate grey hyperpigmentation on exposed areas), busulphan, gold and silver).

Remember other causes of raised ACTH (Nelson's syndrome, ectopic ACTH).

Popular examination causes include uraemia (clues are anaemia and brown line on nails +/- presence of AV fistula on arms), haemochromatosis (see p. 31), primary biliary cirrhosis (typically middle-aged lady with prominent scratch marks and xanthelasmata) and porphyria cutanea tarda. Clues in the latter are scarring on face, neck, forearms, hands, +/- increased skin fragility, erythema, vesicles, bullae, hirsutism. Alcohol-related liver disease commonly associated; urinary uroporphyrins raised, especially in attacks; similar skin changes may occur in variegate porphyria.

Notes

DIABETES MELLITUS

Revise the patterns of abnormal signs which may occur and devise a scheme of examination for complications (including skin, feet, eyes (especially fundi), peripheral neuropathy and examination for vascular complications) in case this is asked.

Notes

ACROMEGALY

The candidate is usually asked to look at either the hands or face.

Look for and be ready to comment on the typical features: large hands with broad, spatulate fingers, large lips and nose, prominent supraorbital ridges, protrusion of the lower jaw (prognathism). Look at the skin for evidence of seborrhoea, excessive sweating, acne or hirsutism.

Ask to see the patient's tongue (it may be enlarged, with impressions formed by teeth on the edges), and ask him to clench his teeth; look for dental malocclusion. NB. Other causes of large tongue are amyloidosis (primary), cretinism, mongolism.

Now proceed (with examiner's permission) to test for bitemporal hemianopia and optic atrophy. Look for kyphosis (vertebral enlargement occurs) and test for carpal tunnel syndrome.

Tell the examiner that you would like to measure the patient's blood pressure (elevated in 15%) and test the urine for glucose (diabetes mellitus in 10%, impaired glucose tolerance in 20%).

Other signs which could be looked for include enlargement of the thyroid, heart, liver and spleen, and presence of arthropathy of large joints (due to degenerative arthropathy and/or chondrocalcinosis).

Gynaecomastia and/or galactorrhoea may also occur.

Always say that you would like to see old photographs of the patient (these are often brought along specially).

Notes

DISORDERS OF THE REPRODUCTIVE SYSTEM

HIRSUTISM

Revise the causes of hirsutism. Remember that pathological changes – virilisation, rather than physiological variation – are suggested by deepening of the voice, temporal baldness, breast atrophy and clitoral hypertrophy.

Revise the features of primary and secondary hypogonadism in males and females. Revise the features of Turner's syndrome.

Notes

PAGET'S DISEASE

You will usually be presented with a 'bowed tibia'. Bowing may be anterior and laterally (NB. Lateral bowing occurs in rickets, forward bowing (sabre tibia) in syphilis. Palpate the bone for increased temperature.

Look at the patient's head for the typical skull appearances. After checking for skeletal changes elsewhere, you may ask if you may look for complications such as deafness, optic atrophy or angioid streaks, cardiac failure (high output), cord compression (due to basilar invagination), root lesions due to vertebral damage. Other complications include fractures, immobilisation hypercalcaemia, sarcomatous changes (1–2%), osteoarthritis of related joints.

Notes

MARFAN'S SYNDROME (AUTOSOMAL DOMINANT)

You will usually be asked to look at the patient's hands. Once you have made a diagnosis, be ready to continue with a prepared scheme of examination: check for a high arched palate, lens dislocation (upwards) aortic regurgitation and mitral valve prolapse. (Remember dissecting aneurysm is also associated.) Look for scoliosis.

Note that in homocystinuria (which also causes arachnodactyly) there is mental retardation, downward lens dislocation, vascular thromboses, osteoporosis and homocystine in the urine.

Notes

KLINEFELTER'S SYNDROME

Revise the features of this condition. Remember that the patient with the classical form will have eunuchoidal proportions (span more than 5 cm greater than height; sole to symphysis pubis greater than symphysis pubis to crown); patients are generally tall.

The testes are small and firm (ask permission from both patient and examiners before examining these) and there is a varying degree of hypogonadism; look for poor muscular development and diminished facial, axillary and pubic hair growth.

Gynaecomastia is usually present (you should check that true gynaecomastia is present and not just fat deposition). Revise the other causes of gynaecomastia; commoner causes include:

- Drugs (e.g. spironolactone, oestrogens, digitalis, cimetidine)
- Hepatic cirrhosis (especially alcoholic)
- Bronchial carcinoma
- Testicular teratoma
- Paraplegia

Revise the rarer causes and have a scheme for investigation of gynaecomastia.

Notes

PSEUDOHYPOPARATHYROIDISM

On rare occasions this may be shown as a short case. You may be asked to look at the hands (short or absent fourth metacarpal). Learn the features just in case.

Notes

OTHER METABOLIC BONE DISEASES

As stated in the PACES guidelines, you must revise and be able to discuss the pathophysiology of other metabolic bone diseases including osteoporosis, hyper and hypoparathyroidism, Paget's disease and abnormalities of bone development (including achondroplasia and rickets or osteomalacia).

Notes

PARTIAL LIPODYSTROPHY

A rare short case. There is loss of subcutaneous fat from the face and arms.

The condition is associated with mesangiocapillary glomerulonephritis.

Notes

6.4 EYES

Revise the various pupillary defects (see section on pupillary abnormalities p. 75)

'EXAMINE THIS MAN'S EYES'

1. Observe for presence of:

- Exophthalmos
- Ptosis
- Squint
- Xanthelasmata
- Arcus
- Corneal calcification
- Blue sclerae
- Kayser-Fleischer rings
- Thyroidectomy scar (always check for this as it gives a strong clue as to the presence of thyroid eye disease)

2. Test visual acuity in both eyes using pocket reading chart.

    If patient wears glasses these should be worn to correct for refractive errors.

3. Test eye movements (ask patient to follow white hat pin with his eyes and to report any double vision).

    Observe at the same time for nystagmus, both horizontal and vertical. Diplopia and nystagmus are such common short cases that I recommend testing for them at this early stage.

4. Test visual fields

    Quickly check for visual inattention using fingers. Then test visual fields in each eye using white hat pin.

5. Examine pupils

    Observe for dilatation, constriction or irregularity.
    Test reactions to light and accommodation. (Beware the glass eye which reacts to neither!)

6. Examine the fundi checking first for the red reflex.

    Ask the examiner whether he wishes you to examine the corneal reflex.

FUNDI

Revise the following popular examination cases by sketching the characteristic appearances in the spaces below:

a) Diabetic retinopathy   – proliferative   b) Malignant
                            – background   hypertension

c) Optic atrophy   d) Choroiditis   e) Retinitis
                                         pigmentosa

f) Retinal artery   g) Retinal vein   h) Angioid streaks
   thrombosis   thrombosis

i) Senile macular   j) Papilloedema   k) Glaucoma
   degeneration

Notes on fundi

a) Diabetes: you will be expected to comment on whether the retinopathy is background or proliferative. Remember that in the latter condition as well as new vessel formation, there may be the complications of vitreous haemorrhage, fibrous tissue formation, retinal detachment and rubeosis iridis (which may in turn lead to glaucoma). Laser burns will often be present.

b) Hypertensive retinopathy: the case will usually be of malignant hypertension. Revise the Keith, Wagener and Barber classification (less used now than before, but you may be expected to know it):

Grade 1.   Arteriolar narrowing/silver-wiring

Grade 2.   AV nipping

Grade 3.   Haemorrhages + exudates — soft / hard

Grade 4.   As for 3, but with papilloedema

c) Optic atrophy: divide the cases into:

Primary   (direct damage to nerve, e.g. post-neuritic, optic nerve compression, ischaemic, traumatic, toxic, infective (e.g. syphilis), malnutritional or hereditary (e.g. Leber's): disc is very pale with distinct lamina cribrosa;

Secondary   (after papilloedema): the disc is grey-white with indistinct edges and lamina cribrosa.

Consecutive   to retinal disease, e.g. retinitis pigmentosa, choroiditis.

d) Choroiditis: irregular areas of white sclera with dark patches of pigment-epithelium. NB. Laser burns may give similar appearance. Toxoplasmosis is a common and important cause: revise the others.

e) Retinitis pigmentosa: be sure that you can recognise this classic case. As well as occurring as an isolated abnormality, it may be associated with a variety of hereditary syndromes e.g.

• Laurence Moon-Biedl (polydactyly, obesity, mental retardation)

- Refsum's disease (see p. 83). There may be concentric field constriction; NB. Night vision is lost early.

f) Retinal artery thrombosis remember that a 'cherry red spot' may be seen at the macula (choroid visible through this retina) from one to two days after the occlusion: in late cases there is optic atrophy. Revise the associations.

g) Retinal vein occlusion branch or central vein occlusions may be shown. In the latter there may be papilloedema.

h) Angioid streaks occur classically in pseudoxanthoma elasticum. Look for chicken-skin lesions on the neck: yellowish papules forming plaques with loss of elasticity. Axillae, elbows and groins are other sites for these. They may also occur in Paget's disease and sickle-cell anaemia. The defect is in Bruch's membrane.

i) Senile macular degeneration: macula may be mottled with pigment or swollen with exudate or contain haemorrhagic residues.

j) Papilloedema: revise the progressive changes occurring in its development (see Patten p.43). Note that the disc may appear pink in optic neuritis, but in this case there is usually marked loss of visual acuity and pain on moving the eye.

k) Glaucoma: the deeply cupped disc may be shown. Remember that cupping and pallor may occur in myopia, while hypermetropia may cause small, pink discs (pseudopapilloedema).

Notes

7. THE EXAMINATION DAY

The clinical part of the Membership examination is held in a variety of centres and it is worth spending some time planning how you will get to your particular hospital. Amazingly, there are always candidates who arrive late, sweating profusely and gasping for breath after running up several flights of stairs. It is impossible to appear suitably composed in this state. Your body may be ready for fight or flight but neither of these is suitable behaviour in the Membership examination!

Arrive, therefore, in plenty of time: *at least* half an hour before the starting time. You will be given some forms to fill in and can also use the extra time to smarten yourself up and check that your instruments are arranged in your pockets so that you can find them without fumbling.

You must pay careful attention to your appearance in the examination.

It is advisable to dress conservatively. For men a dark suit and white shirt, a plain (not club) tie and dark shoes are appropriate; hair should be short. Women should also opt for sober and sensible clothes.

Smell should be neutral: spicy food and alcohol should be avoided for at least a day before the examination.

You will meet different types of examiners, some more aggressive, others more benign. The golden rule in all cases is to be polite and courteous at all times. Even if you feel that you are being harassed you must not appear upset or argue: you will achieve nothing by doing this. If one examiner seems to be adopting a rather aggressive approach the other may be sympathetic to you and it is well known for candidates to pass even after a difficult time. In fact you will often receive little or no feedback on whether what you are saying is right or wrong, but you must not let this put you off.

Another trap to avoid is that of being pushed into changing your mind over a diagnosis or fact about which you are reasonably certain. Examiners who ask 'Are you sure?' are by no means always implying that you are wrong.

This is completely different from the situation in which an examiner tells you that something you have said is wrong. Never argue in this situation, even if you think you are right.

It is easy to give stupid answers when under pressure. If you do this and realise it then be sure to retract that statement at once and say that you know that it was wrong. This is much better than letting the examiners think that you are incompetent. Similarly if you know nothing about a topic about which you are being asked you should admit this at once to avoid wasting time or giving an answer which is false or dangerous.

Try to think positively at all stages of the examination. It is your show and every minute must be spent in trying to convince the examiners that you will be a worthy member of their College. There is very little time in which to do this and you must give the maximum concentration to the task for the whole period of the examination. The candidate who appears fully alert is more likely to capture the examiners' attention. They will know more than you about their subject and you may well learn something during the examination. You are not expected to be a specialist yet.

Finally, it is sometimes claimed that there is a large element of luck in how you get on in the clinical. This tends to be exaggerated, particularly by those who fail. If you have prepared carefully and thoroughly, the dice will be loaded heavily in your favour.

REFERENCES

1. *MRCP (UK) Part 2 Clinical Examination (PACES) and Clinical Guidelines 2001/2* edition, MRCP(UK) Central Office, Royal Colleges of Physicians of the United Kingdom

2. Hope, T (2000), Consent in 'Ethics and Communication Skills', *Medicine* Vol 28:10, pp 5–9 The Medicine Publishing Company Ltd

3. Alderson, P and Goodey, C (1998), Theories of Consent. *BMJ* 317: 1313–1315

4. Apollo, *The Human Face of Medicine* (2001) 2-CD distance learning program, BMJ Publishing Group, London

5. Orme-Smith, A and Spicer, J, *Ethics in General Practice*, Radcliffe Medical Press, 2001

6. Lockwood, G (2000) Confidentiality in 'Ethics and Communication Skills', *Medicine* Vol 28:10, pp 10–12, The Medicine Publishing Company Ltd

7. Campbell, A, Charlesworth, M, Gilett, G and Jones, G (1997), *Medical Ethics*, Second Edn, Oxford University Press

8. Savulescu, J (2000) End-of-life decisions; in 'Ethics and Communication Skills', *Medicine* Vol 28:10, pp 13–16, The Medicine Publishing Company Ltd

9. Purtilo, R (1999), *Ethical Dimensions in the Health Professions*, W.B.Saunders Company, Philadelphia

10. Patten, J (1995), *Neurological Differential Diagnosis* – 2nd Edition, Springer Verlag, Berlin

11. *'Withholding and withdrawing life sustaining treatment from elderly people: towards formal guidelines.'* Doyal, L and Wilsher, D, BMJ 308:1689–1692

12. Parsons, M and Johnson, M (2001), *Diagnosis in Color: Neurology*, Mosby, Edinburgh

REVISION INDEX